CRADLE OF MANKIND

A view of South Island and
the south shores from The Barrier.

Overleaf: Panorama of Suguta Valley
showing the Cathedral Rock landmark and the
alkaline residue of Lake Logipi.

CRADLE OF MANKIND

MOHAMED AMIN

With a Foreword by
Richard Leakey

Chatto & Windus

LONDON : 1981

Commentary: Brian Tetley

Anthropology: Alan Earnshaw

Design: Craig Dodd

First Published 1981 by
Chatto & Windus Ltd
40 William IV Street · London WC2N 4DF

*

Clarke Irwin & Co Ltd · Toronto

British Library Cataloguing in Publication Data
Amin, Mohamed
　Cradle of mankind.
1. Lake Rudolf region (Kenya) – Social life and customs
　I. Title
967.6′2704　　DT434.T/

ISBN 0-7011-2587-X

© Mohamed Amin and Camerapix 1981

This book was designed and produced by
Camerapix,
P.O. Box 45048,
Nairobi, Kenya.

MAPS BY SURVEY OF KENYA.
RIFT VALLEY MAP BY OXFORD UNIVERSITY PRESS.

Filmset by Keyspools Ltd, England.
Printed in Italy by Arnoldo Mondadori Editore, Verona.

Frontispiece: View of South Island from Loiyangalani. The camels in the
foreground blend naturally against the island's hummock-backed silhouette.

CONTENTS

Acknowledgements

I would like to thank all those who have generously helped me in the years from 1968 when I first visited Lake Turkana, the Chiefs and the people of the el-Molo, Samburu, Turkana, Rendille, Gabbra and Merille who allowed me to stay with them. In particular I am grateful to Moses Mayo Lenairoshi of Samburu County Council and Chief Simon Peter Lekarikei, Paul Toulmin-Rothe and Bob McConnell: to Dr Anne Spoerry and Sister Sean Underwood of East African Flying Doctors Service, Father Redento Tignonsini of Korr and Father Joseph Polet of Loiyangalani.

Special thanks are due to Peter Moll, Stewart Sommerlad, Andrew Johnson, Gavin Bennett, and Saidi Suleiman Salim who were all members of my team for the 1980 Round Turkana Expedition; also to Alan Earnshaw for his anthropological research, to Brian Tetley for writing the commentary and Graham Hancock for editing the manuscript.

Grateful acknowledgement is also made to all the people who helped the Expedition and in the production of this book: Richard and Dr Meave Leakey, John Eames, John McHaffie, P. A. Clarke, Bob Smith, Robert Caulkwell and Mary Anne Fitzgerald for reading the manuscript and making suggestions.

Thanks are also due to Guy Bromley, Jay Smith, Jake Grieves-Cook, Keith Ayton, Millar Cuthbert, S. J. Fabian, Hugh Lionnet, J. P. Lebrun, Chum van Someren, Noel Kennaway, Martin Pickford, Kamoya Kimeu, Mike Badger, Mike Somerton-Rayner and many others for their encouragement and assistance.

My particular thanks to the Ministries of Information of Kenya and Ethiopia, the Kenya National Archives, and the National Museums of Kenya for their invaluable assistance; and to my secretary Mrs Joyce Mbao for typing the manuscript. The Survey of Kenya, too, deserve thanks for preparing seven of the eight maps used in this book and for advising on the spelling of place names.

Finally, I owe much to the unfailing support of my wife Dolly and son Salim through all the long hours of work.

Mohamed Amin

Previous page: Beyond the volcanic mass of Emuru Ngogolak (foreground) stand two craters which may form part of the volcanic cluster which includes Losetom in the South of the Suguta. The parallel vents on either slope of the far crater emit powerful jets of carbon dioxide from a fault deep in the earth. The base of the crater contains water varying in tone according to the level of its algae content. The appearance of the outer base is the result of water lapping around the crater during the centuries that it lay in a now vanished lake. The horizon shows Emuru Akirim and the Lolilia Gorge below the Lopet Plateau.

Overleaf: The waterline etched around the outer and inner crescent rim of Kakorinya Crater (left) testifies that centuries ago all this area was once part of a larger and much deeper Lake Logipi. To the right of the picture is Andrew's Volcano, so named by H. S. H. Cavendish after his young companion Lieutenant H. Andrew during an expedition in 1897.

Foreword

MY OWN EXPERIENCES WITH LAKE TURKANA BEGAN IN 1968 WHEN I JOURNEYED overland to explore the eastern shores in search of fossils that I hoped might tell us more about Man's origins in prehistory. From the first moment I saw the lake, I knew that it would be a lasting love as indeed it has been. I know of no other place where I would prefer to be. My family and I continue to spend whatever time we can at Koobi Fora, where I have a research base and a simple, happy home. Turkana is a splendid lake, constantly changing in colour and surrounded by a stark but beautiful landscape. No words can adequately describe this marvellous area. To the casual visitor it may seem harsh and forbidding, but this is a mask that conceals the real character which is beneath and much more subtle.

Lake Turkana has a very long history and extensive scientific investigations have now been carried out in a number of areas surrounding it. We know that the present body of water is a remnant, almost a ghost, of a much larger lake which existed in some form for several million years before the present. Throughout this period, an amazing diversity of animal life has flourished near the shores. From the study of fossils, a complex picture of the lake's many phases is now being drawn and understood.

Some of the most important events in our own evolution occurred gradually over this period of several million years and many of the details are known now as a result of discoveries from deposits of prehistoric Lake Turkana. There has been extensive work in the Omo Valley at the northern end of the lake. Similar work is continuing along the eastern shore at Koobi Fora and, more recently, studies have begun along the western shore. The living fauna and flora of Lake Turkana is being studied and the ecology of the lake itself is now minutely detailed. The people who live around the lake are also well known and all have been successfully integrated into the Kenya of the 1980s and the nation's commitment to modernisation.

Lake Turkana remains a place where misconceptions are frequent and fables abound. Several books have been written and more will surely follow as increasing numbers of people are caught by the magic of this extraordinary place. I hope that this book, with its excellent illustrations and provocative text, will provide many with the appreciation of the real unmasked Lake Turkana, the one I know. It is a lake with a fantastic history – a water that has nurtured extraordinary events and a place that even today seems spellbound.

Richard Leakey
Director/Chief Executive
National Museums of Kenya

LAND OF GENESIS

The Story of a Lake

IF YOU TAKE A CURVED LINE ON THE MAP, HALFWAY BETWEEN THE modern cities of Addis Ababa and Nairobi, you will find a long, narrow stretch of water in one of Africa's most remote regions. Its shores are believed to be the place where man's ancestors took their first faltering footsteps more than two million years ago in what is now known as the 'Cradle of Mankind'.

Two Austrians, Count Samuel Teleki von Szek and Lieutenant Ludwig von Hohnel, were probably the first white travellers to look on it less than a century ago. The road is still much the same as when they travelled along it – a dusty track that winds through mountain valleys and over old volcanoes to the crest of a hill. The lake comes into view from the top of that hill – suddenly and unexpectedly.

This 2,500-square mile stretch of water, alkaline and barely drinkable, is capricious. Sometimes it is calm and unruffled, often it is turbulent with an impression of malevolence. From the hilltop vantage point, however, the lake stretches away peacefully enough into the distance, its shimmering surface sometimes taking on the colour and even the texture of jade.

As von Hohnel described it on March 6, 1888, heaven could present no fairer view: 'We hurried as fast as we could to the top of our ridge, the scene gradually developing itself as we advanced, until an entirely new world was spread out before our astonished eyes. The void down in the depths beneath became filled as if by magic with picturesque mountains and rugged slopes, with a medley of ravines and valleys, which appeared to be closing up from every side to form a fitting frame for the dark-blue gleaming surface of the lake stretching away as far as the eye could reach.

'For a long time we gazed in speechless delight, spellbound by the beauty of the scene before us, whilst our men, equally silent, stared into the distance for a few minutes presently to break into shouts of astonishment at the sight of the glittering expanse of the great lake which melted on the horizon into the blue of the sky'.

They gave the Jade Sea a new and foreign name – 'Rudolf' after their Austrian Prince. But posterity in Africa is brief. Before a century was out the Government of independent Kenya had rechristened the lake, naming it 'Turkana' after one of the tribes who live on its shores.

Lake Turkana lies in a once uncharted wilderness north of the Equator. This is a land of warring, nomadic desert tribesmen and their herds, bordered at its northernmost point by Sudan and Ethiopia. Little more than 9,000 years ago, however, Lake Turkana stretched at least another hundred miles southwards. It is

Previous page: Lava outcrops,
spiky and jagged, mark the descent from the
3,500 foot Barrier to Suguta Valley.

14

one of the largest of the lakes scattered along Africa's Great Rift Valley, the 3,500 mile flaw that extends from the Danakil Plains of Ethiopia on the Red Sea to Beira in Mozambique.

The Rift lakes appear on the map as part of a connected chain. Eduard Suess, an Austrian geologist, made the first significant deduction from this chain in 1891. Although Suess had never been to Africa, he concluded from the accounts of both Teleki and von Hohnel that Lake Rudolf was a link in a line from Lake Nyasa in the south to the River Jordan in the north caused by a series of movements in the earth's surface.

These movements – by throwing up exposed sedimentary layers which can be precisely dated and which have preserved prehistoric fossils in a remarkably good state – have given Lake Turkana an enduring significance for researchers. From a temporary settlement of wooden huts on one of its sandy shores, at a place called Koobi Fora, scientists of many disciplines are today combining intuition with evidence to reconstruct stone-age events of more than two million years ago. The aim, as one of them says, is to determine 'just what it was that made us human'.

The extent of the operations at Lake Turkana is immense and discovery has been on a similarly grand scale. Thirteen years of sifting through a thousand square miles of fossil-rich sites has pushed back our knowledge of Man's beginnings more than a million years.

Most of the sites, under the care of the National Museums of Kenya, fall within the recently established Sibiloi National Park. The park supports a surprisingly large variety of wildlife on its 388,000 protected acres: oryx; Grant's gazelle; Grevy's and Burchell's zebra; lion; cheetah; leopard and hyena; as well as topi and other smaller species.

It was Major Ian Grimwood, then Kenya's Chief Game Warden, who in the early 1960s conceived the idea of this lakeside reserve. He hoped that in such a remote area, without conflict with human interests, these species would be less prone to the depredations of Man. Grimwood's plans came to fruition long after his term of office. Sibiloi was established as a national park in 1973. As the 1980s dawned it remained what he had hoped it would be: a place where the rarer species would be 'perpetually inviolate'. But is there such a thing as perpetuity in Africa, or in the world?

Around Lake Turkana all is the same, yet all is change. Strong winds blow almost continuously at Koobi Fora, gusting gale force seven to ten. The temperature exceeds 100 degrees Fahrenheit and the natural rate of soil erosion is alarming.

Change, when it comes, is swift and stunning. Until recently the whole of the Turkana hinterland supported large elephant herds. The million-year-old bones of their ancestors lie in Koobi Fora's soil. But no elephants have been seen at the lake since the late 1930s. Before that they were abundant, and certainly so in Teleki's time. The Austrian made his own small contribution to their departure. Though an appalling marksman, he managed on one occasion for instance to shoot five elephants in a day. One had tusks weighing 229 pounds.

The exodus of the elephants is symbolic of a wider truth. Lake Turkana, shaped like a finger with too many knuckles, is in reluctant conflict with the twentieth century. Its remoteness proves daily to be less and less of a protection for its fragile ecology. Modern roads are being bulldozed through the western region, and microwave stations are following the same course. And at Kalokol, near Ferguson's Gulf on the western shores, the Norwegian Government has built a large fish-processing plant, proving that there are no barriers to the industrial revolution.

Inevitably the new influences will also crowd in upon the proud people of the lake whose way of life is still as near to untouched primitive existence as any in Africa.

The often fierce tribes use much the same techniques as our nomadic ancestors from Biblical days. 'For peoples who are pastoral,' says Colin Willock in *Africa's Rift Valley*, 'with social organisations based on communal grazing land and water supplies, the problems of living in a region where rainfall is erratic and grazing

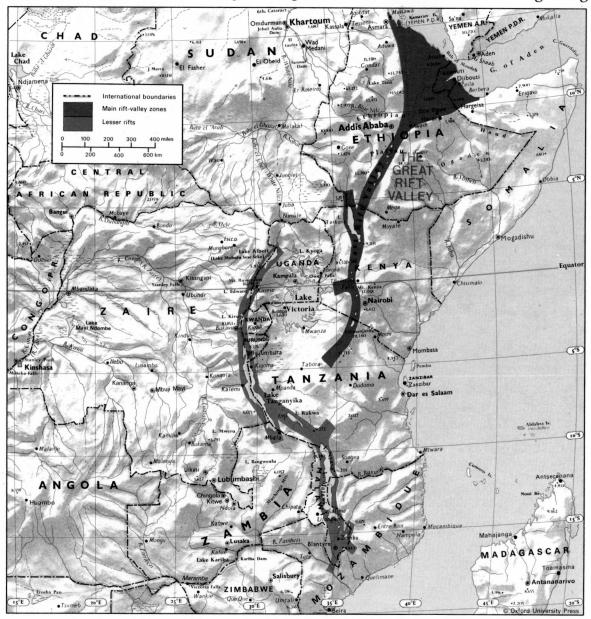

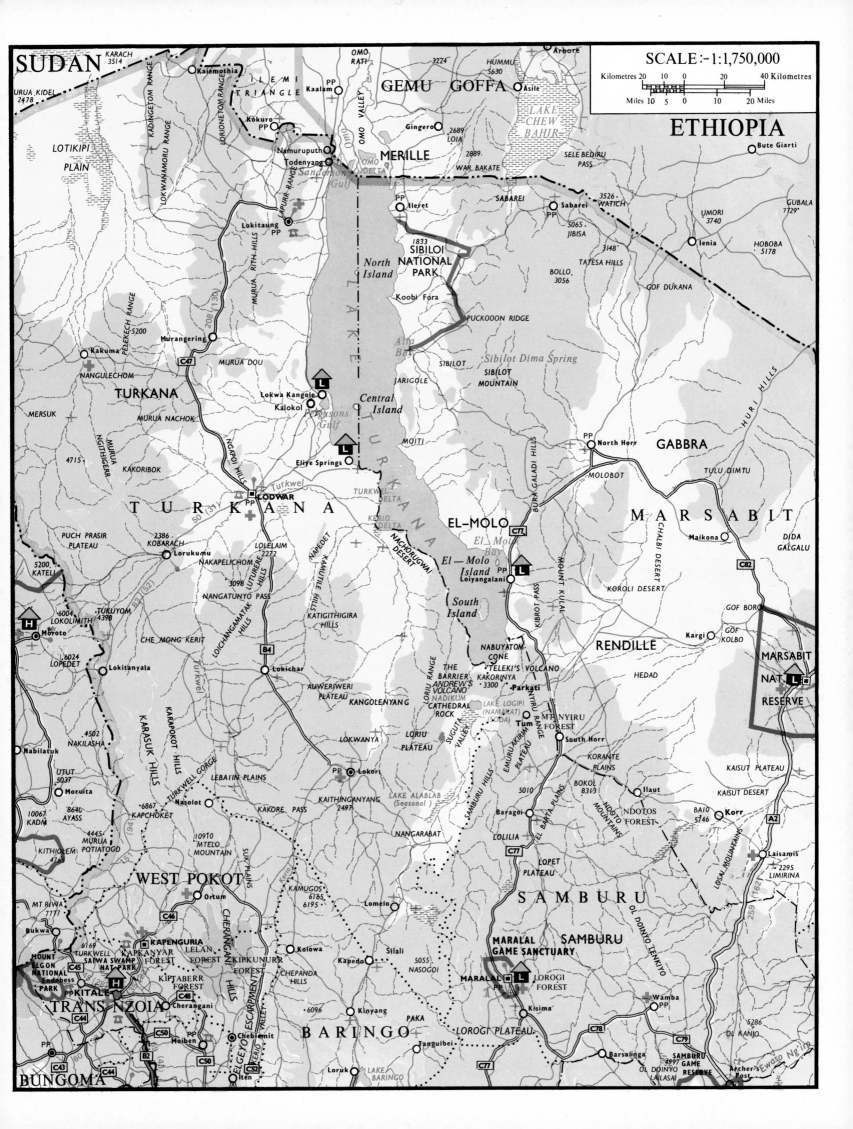

land sparse are almost insuperable.' Almost, but not quite. Few people anywhere in the world today, or in any era, have come to terms with a melancholy environment to the degree of harmony achieved by these communities.

For centuries these badlands – stretching from what is now Uganda's Karamoja and Acholi provinces in the West to Sudan's Equatorial and Jonglei provinces in the north – have provided a meagre living for nomads and their herds in search of browsing and of stock to steal. Across this featureless plain, claimed by no state or chief, the Nilotic people migrated into Kenya and Tanzania centuries ago, some to settle around Lake Turkana. There is a touch of resolution, a determined conservatism, an active indifference to other ways, and an affinity with their land which marks all these semi-desert tribes.

THE FORCES which fragmented the Rift Valley and formed its lakes also created a string of volcanoes running along the valley floor in Ethiopia, Kenya and Tanzania. Such volcanoes are to be found in Lake Turkana, and on the south shore. They form part of a line, ending near Lake Natron, which includes Silali, Paka, Menengai, Longonot, Susua and in Tanzania Ol Doinyo Lengai, the Maasai *Mountain of God* which last erupted in 1966.

This volcanic activity began more than twenty million years ago and its implicit ferocity still evokes a sense of grandeur. Not one of the Rift volcanoes can be said to be extinct – in 1928 an earthquake along the same fault split the earth's crust six feet for a length of several miles somewhere between Lake Baringo and Solai below the Laikipia plains.

There was certainly enough evidence to suggest some dramatic upheaval at the end of the last century when von Hohnel named a still-smoking volcano after his leader Count Teleki – a volcano that later visitors had difficulty in finding.

Arthur Mortimer Champion, then the Provincial Commissioner in Lodwar, declared in 1932: 'It was obviously one of my duties to put an end to this mystery.' He made a foot safari to the south to find Teleki's Volcano and, at the same time, explored the Suguta Valley which lies 400 feet below Lake Turkana's 1,230-foot shore level. Thousands of years ago the Valley formed part of the lake but today a 3,500-foot volcanic massif called The Barrier dams the lake's waters and prevents them tumbling into this natural inferno where temperatures reach 140 degrees Fahrenheit.

Volcanic eruptions also raised the lake's three main islands. The largest, thirty square miles of rock called South Island which lies four miles off the east coast and fifteen miles from the south coast, is covered with ash almost from end to end. The ghostly glow of its luminous vents at night inspired stories of evil spirits among the el-Molo tribe who live near Loiyangalani on the south-east shore.

There is more than a touch of whimsical imagination in this superstition. Others have shared it. 'The feeling of a landscape always on the move,' insinuated itself on Willock, 'constantly rearranging itself according to some unfathomable plan.' And discrepancies in travellers' accounts after Teleki's visit confirm tribal stories of the island being overwhelmed by tidal waves following massive eruptions and earth movements.

There is also a minor human tragedy associated with South Island. Its first known European visitors were members of an expedition led by Vivien Fuchs, later knighted for his exploratory work in Antarctica. Three days after landing on the island Fuchs returned to the mainland, sending Dr S. W. Dyson to join W. H. R. Martin on the island on July 28, 1934. Dyson, the expedition's health officer, collected the zoological specimens. Martin, a surveyor who was also a qualified forester, collected the botanical specimens. Fuchs gave explicit orders for them to return to the mainland by August 13 at the latest. They were never seen again.

Fuchs organised one of the first air-ground searches in East Africa, planes flying out from Nairobi's Wilson Airport and combing the island and lake shores. Fuchs himself was prevented by bad light, rough weather and mechanical problems from getting ashore by boat. He was on the water eight days and blamed the colonial government for ordering him to sail along the western extremity when he could have travelled south under the lee of the east coast. His boat sank once and had to be refloated.

No traces were found on South Island which might have given a clue to the fate of the two men. 'Lack of petrol and supplies,' records Fuchs, 'forbade that we make another attempt; so ended our search for any signs of what had caused the accident to our two companions. During the search two tins, two oars and Dyson's hat were found on the west shores of the lake, the latter being nearly seventy miles north of what must have been the scene of the accident.'

Should Fuchs have given up the search so soon? There had to be some lingering trace, perhaps only the remains of a camp fire, to cast some light on the last moments of Dyson and Martin. As it is, not even a simple stone obelisk or cairn perpetuates the memory of South Island's two known victims.

Fuchs was handicapped, of course, by lack of a suitable craft. The crossing to the island was made in a collapsible wooden boat – not the vessel for waters which British sailors forty years later said were 'rougher than the North Sea'.

FEW SIZEABLE ships or boats have ever sailed on Lake Turkana and the fate of those that have gives credence to ecologist Alistair Graham's belief that 'no one had meddled with Lake Rudolf without paying for it one way or another'.

The first European-owned boat on these waters was also the first to sink. It was made of canvas and belonged to Teleki. It was destroyed by a wounded and angry elephant which had sought refuge in the shallows. The boat and crew had been despatched to finish the beast.

The first large vessel to sail the lake was a Bermuda-rigged schooner called *Patricia* captained by an ex-Royal Naval officer, Morris Vernon. Built by the Public Works Department in Mombasa, it was shipped in parts, each numbered for easy assembly, by rail to Thika and overland by oxcart and porters. With two 30-foot masts, lee boards instead of keel and sails of khaki drill, *Patricia* did not linger long on the Jade Sea. She ran aground off the mouth of the seasonal Kerio river during her maiden voyage in 1923. Refloated, she later broke loose from her moorings at Loiyangalani, and sank during a gale at the south end of the east coast. The *Patricia* had been intended as a supply ship for contingents of the King's

African Rifles stationed around the lake. In her absence, the army had to revert to victualling by convoys of pack animals.

Another jinx boat was Graham's 19-foot converted lifeboat, hauled overland from Mombasa. This vessel was so unseaworthy it was christened *The Curse* by Bob McConnell, a fishing expert stationed at Ferguson's Gulf in the 1960s. *The Curse* sank three or four times and was fished out each time before committing itself irrevocably to the deep.

McConnell's own boat also foundered, nearly taking him with it. It was a catamaran designed in Mombasa. A wise old hand in the inland base of Kenya's Fisheries Department decided he knew better than the designer and changed its inboard engines for outboards. The catamaran thus shipped water swiftly in a following sea.

The vessels which ply the lake now number about 500 dug-out and fibre-glass canoes belonging to the Turkana fishermen's co-operative which is based at Ferguson's Gulf. There is also the *Halcyon*, an eight-ton Scottish-built trawler belonging to the Fisheries Department. The fleet of canoes and its owners have had disastrous consequences on the ecology of Central Island, another volcanic creation which still emits steam, and which has now been turned into a semi-permanent settlement of Luo and Turkana fishermen. They have begun to slaughter the magnificent Nile crocodiles which until now have traditionally bred on the island. They also kill the birds which breed there and destroy the eggs which they find in nests on the grass-covered volcanic slopes and ledges. More importantly, they are destroying the bushes which provide the wild fruits which support some of the migratory species *en route* from Europe to the Cape.

About three miles across, 800 feet above the lake at its highest point, Central Island has three small internal lakes which the crocodiles use as breeding grounds. For millions of years they have lived in perfect balance with their environment, feeding voraciously on Turkana's teeming fish population, which consists of more than forty species including Nile perch, tilapia, and tiger fish. This natural order has maintained a stable population of about 12,000, the last great colony of crocodiles in the world.

These saurians reach lengths of sixteen feet and have remained unchanged for at least 130 million years. They are survivors of an epoch long before mankind appeared on Turkana's shores. The world owes them something other than extinction.

Almost at the centre of the lake on its north-south axis nine miles from Ferguson's Gulf and fifteen miles from the east coast, Central Island is larger than North Island, forty miles away. No Turkana fishermen camp on this desolate smudge of rock. Instead, the rustle of a resident population of snakes sometimes provides the casual visitor with a sinister sundown lullaby. These reptiles originally drifted down to North Island from the Omo delta on floating islands of papyrus. The Turkana environment is home for some of the world's most poisonous reptiles – saw-scaled vipers and night adders, puff adders and cobras.

The lake offers the same hospitality to a rich variety of bird life: more than 350 species of resident and migratory birds depend on the waters of the Jade Sea for the rich lacustrine life on which they feed. Over the years the spectacle has attracted many ornithologists including Prince Philip the Duke of Edinburgh, and his son, Prince Charles.

WEST OF the Ethiopian capital of Addis Ababa the solid 9,500-foot bulk of Mount Amara climbs out of the highland plateau. Not far from its summit, a small spring bubbles out of the rock and starts its 600-mile journey south.

When it reaches Turkana, swollen by floods and many tributaries, Ethiopia's second largest river, the Omo, cuts a swathe through a twenty-mile wide impenetrable thicket of swamp and papyrus to discharge twenty million cubic metres of life-sustaining water each year into East Africa's fourth largest lake.

The remorseless sun sucks the water out again by intense evaporation. As a result, in the first forty years of this century, Lake Turkana shrank dramatically. Sanderson's Gulf, which in 1902 was thirty miles long and ten miles wide, connected to the main lake by a sound three miles across, reached Namuruputh and beyond. Now it is dry land.

When Fuchs surveyed the western shore in 1934 he found that even two miles out the waters were only eight feet deep. He predicted the northern shores would soon retreat south well inside Kenya. This, of course, has not happened yet; however a 1970s survey confirmed Fuchs's estimate of declining depths at the north end. Part of the problem is that silt from the River Omo is building up the lake bed – some shallows are now only thirty feet deep. Around Central Island, however, and in the far south, depths reach down 300 to 380 feet.

Two other major rivers, the Turkwel and the Kerio, discharge themselves into Lake Turkana. But they are seasonal and have little influence on the lake's major dimensions: it is 180 miles long and 35 miles wide at its maximum.

When the lake was 475 feet deeper many thousands of years ago it was connected to the White Nile basin by an outlet through the Lotikipi Plain beyond Lokitaung and the Murua Rithi Hills. Now all this is part of the semi-desert of thorn scrub which stretches from the foot of the Loriu Plateau in the south to the slopes of the Ethiopian Highlands at Kedada in the north.

Yet if historical perspective has any accuracy the bleak east shore of the lake is the one place on earth which can rightly be regarded as Eden, that lush garden of Biblical legend turned to knife-edge lava wastes and petrified forests. From Ileret in the north to beyond Alia Bay in the south, and inland some twenty miles, the exposed fossil beds at the Koobi Fora site are telling eloquently of what used to be a verdant land which was, perhaps, a true 'Cradle of Mankind'.

Today this land yields little. The soil is worn out. The people hardy, spartan and indifferent to progress. Nothing much counts but human dignity. The only profit is survival: merely staying alive requires considerable resourcefulness and skill.

Left: Nabuyatom Cone on Turkana's south shores. The scarps in the background are evidence of recent earthquake activity. The horizon reveals Mount Nyiru.

Above: Teleki's Volcano, for many years the subject of conjecture and unconfirmed reports that it had erupted and vanished, lies between Lake Turkana's south shore and Suguta Valley. It has not changed since the 1930s when Arthur Mortimer Champion, Turkana Provincial Commissioner, resolved to find it and place it in its proper position on the map. It can be identified inside the large caldera formed when a previous volcano collapsed. The caldera is identifiable as the crescent-shaped scarp in the background.

Top: Barren and deserted, volcanic South Island has an inhospitable appearance. The cove at the north end is one of the few sheltered places on which to beach a craft. The approach is marked by a lava pinnacle which rises nearly 200 feet from the lake bed and is called The Fang. Close by, centuries of accumulated bird guano give crescent-shaped Ekinyang, the visible tip of a submerged crater, a phosphorescent gleam.

Above: A black and yellow bee on Central Island. *Xylocopa aestuans*, the Carpenter Bee recognisable by its yellow thorax, feeds on nectar from the aromatic pink-mauve flower of *Delamerea procumbens*, a monotypic genus. The plant is indigenous to the Turkana area.

Right: Two of the three lakes on the Central Island volcano provide an ideal breeding ground for Nile crocodile. The presence of wandering fishermen has, however, recently driven the crocodiles to seek more secluded places.

Opposite top: This unique boomerang-shaped island near Alia Bay is a favourite haunt of hippos and Nile crocodiles.

Opposite bottom: Close to the headquarters of Sibiloi National Park, a family of crocodiles head for the water. Centuries of isolation have helped keep Lake Turkana's crocodiles safe from hunters. The lake now has the largest remaining population of Nile crocodiles in the world.

Above: Great White Pelicans, *Pelecanus onocrotalus*, take to the air. On the Koobi Fora sand spit beneath them a crocodile slumbers in Turkana's afternoon heat.

More than 350 species of resident and migratory birds make Lake Turkana one of the great ornithological spectacles of the world.

Above: Tawny Eagle, *Aquila rapax*.

Left: Kori Bustard, *Otis kori*.

Opposite top left: Sacred Ibis, *Threskiornis aethiopicus*.

Opposite top right: White Stork, *Ciconia ciconia*.

Opposite bottom left: White-bellied Cormorant, *Phalacrocorax carbo*.

Opposite bottom right: Malachite Kingfisher, *Alcedo cristata*.

Overleaf: Ferguson's Gulf during a rare cloudburst. The early-morning sun bestows an almost romantic aspect on the scene.

CRADLE OF MANKIND

Our Beginning

IT WAS MID-MORNING ONE DAY IN JULY 1967 WHEN RICHARD LEAKEY first flew along the eastern shores of Lake Turkana. Below lay a tangle of blackened sandstone layers that looked like the slag heaps of a coal pit.

Leakey asked the pilot to circle. The single-engined plane turned out over the water beyond the sandy spit of Koobi Fora, to make another pass at a height of one thousand feet.

A camera could only have recorded what was there. Leakey saw things differently, however – not exactly an hallucination but rather an inspired guess, a vision of the distant past as it might have been.

First he saw graceful trees and rolling grasslands where other vegetation also grew. Mischievous monkeys gambolled in the thick foliage. Strange elephant-like pachyderms with shortened trunks and thicker but smaller tusks browsed quietly. Nearby some hairy people, small but upright, with squat low foreheads, chattered amicably in one group; in another workmen banged and chipped stones to fashion new tools.

Then rivers cut through the grasslands in Leakey's inner eye, waters swift and clear. Eden was spread out before him.

EVEN NOW the forces which shaped Africa's Great Rift Valley are not fully understood. The fault was caused by upheavals immense enough to result in a valley that is sometimes thirty miles wide and as much as 2,000 feet deep. It was first investigated by a young Scot, John Walter Gregory. He marched up to Baringo from Mombasa in 1893 and, hammering out samples of different rock layers, he returned to Britain to proclaim his conclusions – that the 3,500-mile long valley was formed 'by the rock sinking in mass, while the adjacent land remained stationary'.

Gregory gave it the name of the Great Rift Valley. But it is the name with which it was endowed by Suess which best captures the imagination: *graben*, deriving from *grabe*, the grave. In the light of what has been found since, no other image could have been more exact.

All along this majestic flaw, in the walls of its great scarps and on or just beneath the surface of its floor, lies evidence of mankind's beginnings. Much of it has yet to be discovered. The assumption that it exists is based on what has been

Previous page: Aerial view of Lake Turkana's
eastern shore between Alia Bay and Koobi Fora.

revealed so far at the two most significant sites in palaeontological history – Olduvai Gorge in Tanzania's Rift Valley and Koobi Fora in Kenya.

Synonymous with both sites is the name of Leakey. Early in the 1960s Drs Louis and Mary Leakey found the 1.8-million-year-old fossil remains of a creature they named *Homo habilis* which means 'Handy Man'. The bones were in the wall of Olduvai Gorge which lies between Lake Natron and Lake Eyasi.

Fewer than ten years later, Louis Leakey's son Richard was summoned by his friend Kamoya Kimeu to a spot on the outlying edges of the Lake Turkana excavations. Richard spent weeks piecing together thirty or more fossil fragments. The result of this painstaking work was another skull similar to that of *Homo habilis* but dating back almost three million years.

Other discoveries of even greater significance have since been made: skulls of the genus *Homo erectus*, the first species of man to walk upright. These discoveries confirm that mankind has been present on earth for at least a million years: 500,000 years longer than was previously believed.

Thereafter, Leakey was often at Koobi Fora, 400 miles north of Nairobi, until a debilitating illness forced him to spend less time there.

TO QUICKEN the pace of discovery, Leakey evolved a new approach to palaeontology involving a multi-disciplinary team of scientists. Doors have been opened to all with the qualities and qualifications to share the work. The result is a unique mix of skills, beliefs and nationalities making more profound assessments about mankind's early history than could ever have been achieved by one person.

When he left school Richard Leakey rebelled against his strong-willed father and vowed he would 'never become a palaeontologist'. Yet surveying Lake Natron in northern Tanzania three years later he found himself unable to resist the tell-tale signs of another rich fossil ground. His parents encouraged him to explore the sedimentary beds and at once Richard struck a fossil lode. In 1964 he assembled a fragment of an *Australopithecus boisei*, an early form of hominid, which had been found by his friend Kamoya. It was a complete jaw and the only specimen in East Africa at that time.

Trapped once again by the Leakey 'manhunting fever' Richard set off for London to complete his formal education catching up on two years of studies in seven months and qualifying for university. But with nine months to wait before the new term opened, he decided to return to Kenya.

There, at the age of 23, he was appointed co-leader of an expedition into southern Ethiopia's Omo Valley. Teams from America, France and Kenya had been allowed to explore rich fossil beds on the river's lower reaches. Leakey joined them and uncovered animal fossils at least four million years old. He also found two *Homo sapiens* skulls which suggested that modern man may have existed as long as 100,000 years ago.

Returning to the site after a visit to Nairobi his pilot flew along Lake Turkana's eastern shores to avoid bad weather. The change of route was another case of 'Leakey's luck'. Borrowing a helicopter from the American Omo Valley team, Richard returned to the sandstone hills near Alia Bay to check on what his inspired vision had promised. The helicopter blades had barely stopped whirling when Leakey picked up a stone-age tool similar to those he had found in Olduvai Gorge as a youngster.

Within months Richard Leakey had assumed the Directorship of Kenya's National Museums and had begun the exploration which was to confirm Koobi Fora's potential as the world's richest treasure-trove of fossils of early hominids.

THE TECTONIC movements which formed the Great Rift Valley established the right formula for preserving fossil bones. Africa's convulsions were spaced over thousands of years, each spasm causing lakes to form and waters to flow along fresh rills and over new-born plains. Each wrack laid down new sediments from these waters, rising in tiers like different fillings in an exotic cake. Tightly compressed in their shrouds of calcium carbonate, within each tier, lay the skeletons of several species including the remains of mankind's ancestors.

Initial discoveries in the Koobi Fora fossil beds are made by surface prospecting – locating areas where erosion has left bones and teeth exposed.

The Rift Valley strata have many prehistoric relics of major importance lying open on the ground. Richard Leakey recounts his discovery of the area's first *Australopithecus* fossil: 'There on the sand twenty feet ahead, in full view beside a thorny bush, lay a domed greyish-white object. Halfway to it I sat down stunned, incredulous, staring. For years I had dreamed of such a prize, and now I had found it – the nearly complete skull of an early hominid'.

Fossil recovery at Koobi Fora is an intricate and delicate task. When a discovery is made a geologist visits the site to determine the exact 'stratigraphic' level in which the fossil lies. This helps to assess the relic's age accurately. The prospectors then scrape down the entire surrounding surface and put it through a sieve in the hope of recovering more fragments. They also keep an eye open for any that might be held tight in the rock.

Different techniques are used to recover fossils that are partly or entirely embedded in rock. The tools are dental picks and brushes made from camels' hair. The samples are so delicate that they can fall apart if touched by the slightest wind. To prevent disintegration, the scientists treat their samples with preservative fluid. Even this has its risks: the impact of a falling drop can break a fossil.

The precise location of each discovery is marked by a concrete post bearing a reference number. The three most important finds are KNM-ER 1470, which is the skull of *Homo habilis*, and KNM-ER 3733 and 3883, the skulls of *Homo erectus*. Visitors to Sibiloi National Park who want to see these sites require special permission from the National Museums of Kenya.

The skulls were rebuilt in the Museum laboratory – rather like solving a three-dimensional jigsaw with missing pieces and without a picture on the box. They are now stored at the Museum Headquarters in Nairobi. Just how significant they are is still being established.

The multi-disciplinary approach which has quickened the pace of evaluation and reconstruction at Koobi Fora includes the relatively new science of taphonomy – the study of what happens to organisms after their death.

Anatomy is another important science. It helps in studying bone formations to find similarities between early and modern man. Thus we know that *Homo erectus* walked on two legs. He was a biped who had some anatomical mechanisms similar to modern man.

Other scientists reconstruct ancient camp sites and learn how to make and use stone-age tools. Others still test sedimentary layers and fossil content to determine an accurate age for each find.

The richest era of discovery dates between three million and one million years ago. In the past decade more than 160 fossil remains of early hominids, more than 4,000 fossil specimens of mammals, and numerous stone-age artefacts have been recovered. The mammal finds include seventy-five extinct and twelve existing species. Other remains include fish, turtle, tortoise and crocodile species.

It is not just the fossils which have given Koobi Fora significance. The sedimentary layers in which the fossils were buried have yielded important evidence of the environment three million years ago and of the animals and plants with which early man and pre-man shared the world.

Leakey believes the layers have provided enough evidence to establish that Lake Turkana's shores were once a well-watered verdant land of forest and grass blessed with an abundance of good things. The plains teemed with wild animals including prehistoric elephants, three-toed ancestors of the horse, sabre-toothed cats, antelopes, giant baboons, rhino-sized pigs, ostriches and many other ancestors of modern species.

And what of the 'missing link', that mythical half-ape, half-man? Richard's father, Louis Leakey, said there was no single missing link. In the search for mankind's origins he believed there would be many. Perhaps this is the case; but each time Richard flies over Koobi Fora one thought nags him: 'Somewhere down there lies the key'.

Until that key is found – if it exists – there are other clues to concern us. If we can learn much from the fossil beds, we can also learn from the nomadic communities who live around the lake's shores – people who have adapted magnificently to their harsh environment and in whose circumstances are to be found reminders of our own beginnings.

Right: Bleached and barren sandstone
wilderness at Koobi Fora. Here on the shores
of Lake Turkana the direct ancestors of modern man may have
taken their first faltering footsteps.

Above and right: The artist Jay H. Matternes has brought Koobi Fora's prehistoric people and animals back to vivid life in these two pictures commissioned by Survival Anglia Ltd. The paintings hang in the National Museum in Nairobi.

Left: This wilderness of black sandstone and remnants of petrified forest was once perhaps the Cradle of Mankind. Here, says an official of the National Museums of Kenya, 'one sees oneself at one instant in time, in a place where millions of years ago events occurred which are still continuing today; the lake rises and the rivers flood, skeletons are buried and preserved as clues which may be exposed again millions of years in the future . . .'

The 1.5-million-year-old fossil remains of a primeval elephant at Koobi Fora.

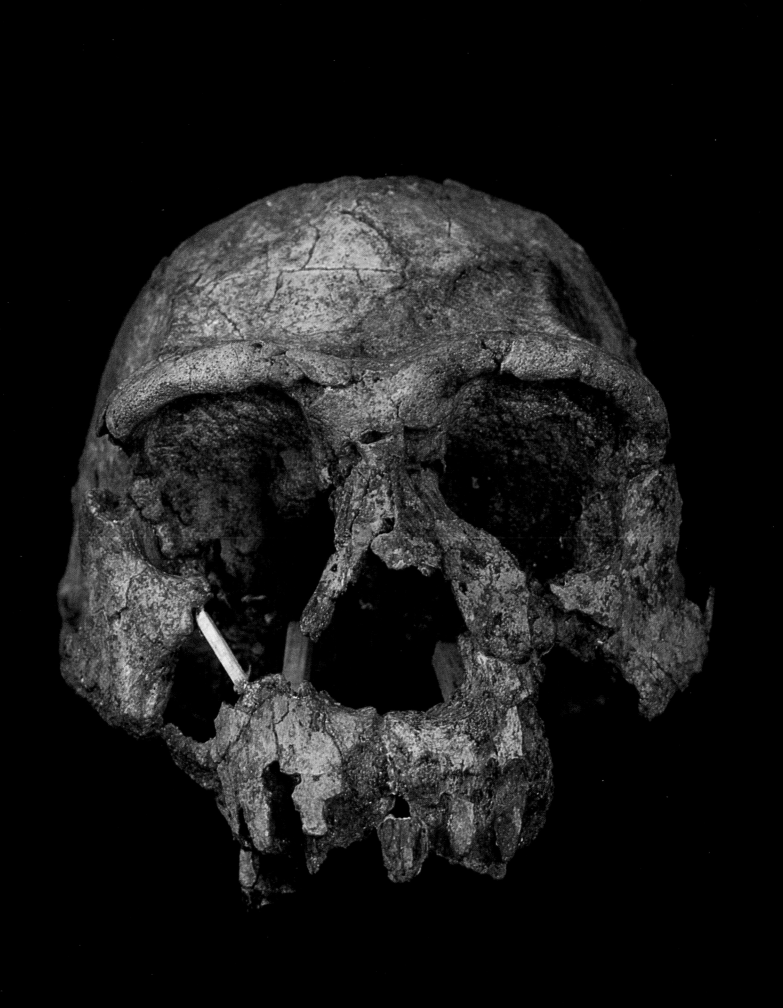

Left: The fossil skull of one of man's oldest known ancestors is listed as KNM-ER 3733 by the National Museums of Kenya and was found at Koobi Fora. It is half a million years older than an example of the same *Homo erectus* species found at Olduvai Gorge, Tanzania. Scientists now suppose from this, and a later find of the same species, KNM-ER 3883, that *Homo erectus* existed for at least a million years. The species is the first known to have walked upright, and heralded modern Man by experiencing a prolonged childhood, and by developing a relatively large brain and small canine teeth. The fragments were painstakingly pieced together by members of the Richard Leakey expedition after their discovery in a fossil bed in the upper section of the Koobi Fora formation.

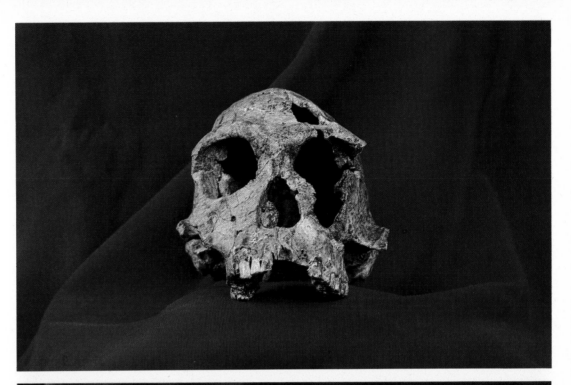

Top right: Skull KNM-ER 1813 found in 1973 by Kamoya Kimeu, is one of the finest reconstructions of *Australopithecus africanus*. Once considered a direct ancestor of modern man, *Australopithecus* is now believed to have shared the Lake Turkana shores with both *Homo habilis* and *erectus*.

Middle right: *Australopithecus boisei*, of which the Skull KNM-ER 406, found near Ileret by Richard and Meave Leakey in 1969, is a fine example. This was a species doomed to quick extinction.

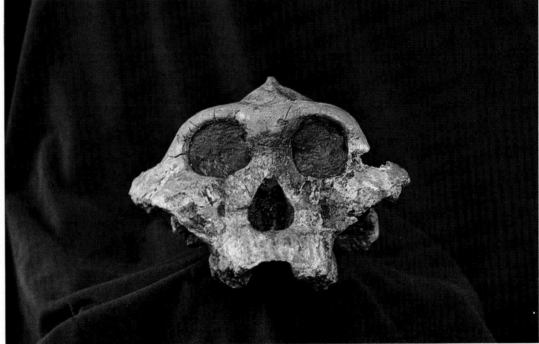

Bottom right: Skull KNM-ER 1470 was the dramatic find which established the potential of the Koobi Fora fossil beds for palaeo-anthropological research. This skull was found as a scattering of fragments by Bernard Ngeneo in 1972 and reconstructed in the laboratory during a period of six weeks by Dr Meave Leakey, Richard Leakey's wife, and an anatomist Alan Walker. It is a specimen of *Homo habilis* more than two million years old. It caused scientists to make a radical revision of long-held views of evolution, a revision speeded up by the subsequent discoveries of the *Homo erectus* fossils.

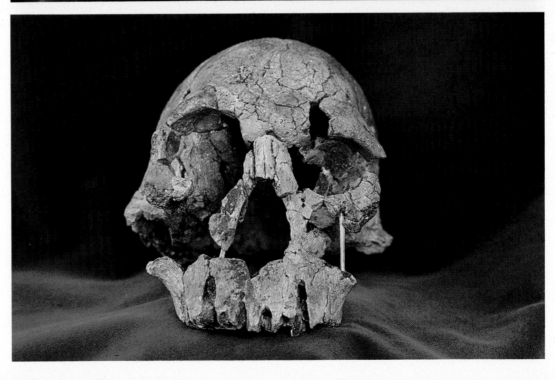

Left: Ostrich on parade in the 388,000 acre Sibiloi National Park.

Above: In the arid wastes of Sibiloi National Park, a shy, long-neck gerenuk rears on its hind legs to find a tasty twig.

Following pages: Stampeding zebra kicking up dust across an arid section of Sibiloi National Park.

Turkana fishermen returning from a night's work as the early-morning sun rises.

SAMBURU

The Proud Warriors

NOT TOO MANY MILES ALONG THE ROAD FROM WHERE THE LAST OF THE
European settlers staked their claim to Kenya's lush highland pastures lie the
moist forests of the 6,000-foot Lorogi Plateau. The settlers coveted the plateau
hopeful of more fertile acres for ranching.

One obstacle barred their way: the 75,000-strong Samburu tribe. The tribe was
formed some centuries ago. Sweeping south in the great Maasai migration, the
Samburu broke away from the main branch to settle in a wedge-shaped triangle
north of Mount Kenya.

The southernmost boundary of Samburu territory today lies just beyond
Rumuruti. Bounded by Mount Kulal in the north, stretching south through

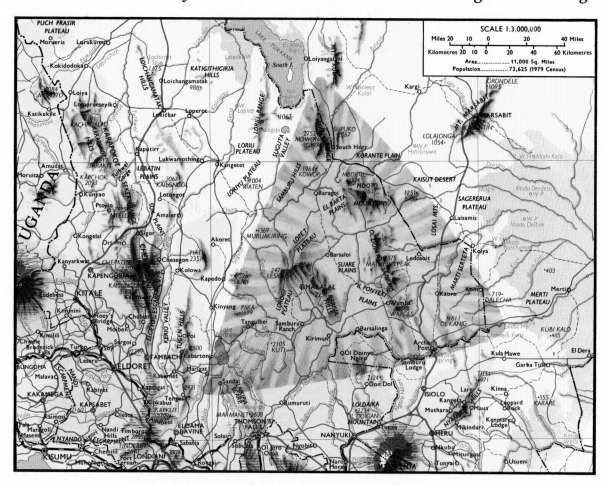

Previous page: Samburu warrior;
the badges of his rank are an oiled skin, ochred hair,
a loose cloth and the spear he carries.

50

Laisamis to the Ewaso Ngiro river and west along this baseline as far as Maralal and the Lorogi Plateau, the Samburu inhabit about 11,000 square miles. In some areas they share a common and remarkably harmonious tenancy with the Rendille – a less affluent tribe. The Rendille are traditional camel nomads, a way of life which contrasts sharply with the Samburu emphasis on cattle ownership.

Von Hohnel was the first European to notice the Samburu's unusual alliance with the Rendille and recorded that the two peoples were 'on the best of terms with each other'. It is a pity that the first European administrators did not heed this observation. They could have saved the Samburu and themselves a great deal of ineffectual argument.

In the event they did not. The Samburu for many years were administered from the heart of white settler country at Nakuru while the Rendille, after some initial friction, were left alone by a more benign administration based in Isiolo. This division of the Samburu and the Rendille could have been very much in the interests of the white settlers who were convinced that the Samburu were over-grazing the potentially rich grasslands which they wanted to take over. The settlers nearly succeeded in their objective; however the bureaucracy, if blundering, never connived. Probably the worst effect of the separation was that it started a quarrel between the Samburu and the colonial administration that was compounded by ignorance of the qualities of Samburu society.

A report of the time typified the rift between the two: 'The Samburu chiefs and headmen are a collection of the most useless and boneless and effete tribal rulers I have had to do with in my experience of fifteen years of Native tribes'. Nonetheless, these same 'useless, boneless and effete rulers' kept the tribal lands from settler hands and furthermore maintained their authority with the young warriors despite predictions to the contrary.

'The existing moran system is now an anachronism,' said a 1930s report, 'which in these days can only lead to trouble as it creates an idle class of irresponsible youths who, deprived of their former work of defending the tribe are bound to get into mischief'.

The administration's attitude persisted. In 1948 cattle raiding had assumed proportions beyond that of simple annoyance. Samburu warriors were, accordingly, press-ganged into a road-building force in an attempt to occupy them more productively. The road they built leads from Baragoi over the lava fields to Tum on the west slopes of Mount Nyiru. The 1948 warriors are now elders and point out the road with great conceit as the best in Samburu.

Several observers have come to regard vanity as a Samburu characteristic. In *Journey to the Jade Sea*, John Hillaby expressed his aggravation at their 'hypertrophy of the ego'. He wrote: 'I sometimes had the impression that they were staring at me but their eyes showed me that they were staring forward and I happened to be in the way.' He believed the Samburu warrior took his leisure so seriously he existed for days on the 'principle of least effort'.

SOMETHING OF the Old Testament's patterns apply to the Samburu society. Senior citizens are not regarded as senile. Age itself is a quality, a gauge of one's ability to survive. Elders, therefore, are not simply respected. They are revered and their judgements have value for, and are valued by, all the community.

Today, as always, though youthful attributes are saluted, youthful arrogance is disdained. The Samburu have developed a subtle hierarchy which maintains this authority. The old and the experienced still decide the community's behaviour.

Social structures are built upon cattle and the ownership of cattle. Pastoralists pure and simple, the Samburu cultivate nothing in the way of cash or food crops. They keep small herds of camels in their northern territory and maintain quite large herds of sheep and goats.

Authorities believe this preference for cattle is justified. Cattle herds are easy to handle and flourish because, within Samburu district, there are areas which offer excellent grazing. Only in the drier northern regions does a halfway group known as the Ariaal Rendille – a mixture of both Samburu and Rendille proper – concentrate on camel breeding. For the majority, however, the damper, higher rangelands militate against camel herds.

Cattle wealth has a profound influence upon Samburu social structure, cattle being everything: property, chattels, money, and the measure of a man's dignity.

During the time of the Samburu's greatest confrontation with settler bureaucracy there was an exchange of views at a hearing of the Carter Land Commission in the 1930s. This exchange provides an insight into Samburu philosophy:

Crown: 'If your cattle go on increasing and the grass gets finished, what will you do?'

Elder: 'I would still keep my cattle. I do not want them to die. I want to look after them. They are our life. As the Government likes shillings, so we Samburu like cattle.'

Crown: 'Would you rather have three hundred cattle or five hundred starving ones?'

Elder: 'I would rather have a thousand starving ones until God gives us grass, because if a man has a lot of cattle, and some die, he still has some left, but if a man has a few cattle and they die, he has none left.'

The biggest cattle holders in Samburu society hold a position parallel to bankers in cash societies. Beasts are loaned in times of hardship on the basis of interest repayment in the form of calves or heifers later.

A man's ability to cope with the traditional demands – gifts, loans or dowries for brides – indicates his social standing. The more cattle he owns the more children he needs to tend them and the more wives he must have to bear these children. Cattle are wealth, wives are wealth. The Samburu word for respect is *nkanyit* and it has a deeper meaning: it is the tribe's single most important element of social courtesy, given in greatest measure to the largest cattle owner. Inevitably this is the man with the most wives and most children.

This craving for respect has created a far-reaching series of social interactions which provide potential for strife for, to maintain their status, the elders cunningly manipulate the tribe's age-set system. Efficiently performed, such manipulations keep a reserve of nubile women on the market longer while the herds expand. The logic is simple: the bigger the herds grow the more dowries the elders can pay. The more dowries they can pay the more wives they can marry. And the more wives they marry the more respect they receive.

The result is that the gap between circumcision and junior elderhood – when the warrior can at last marry – is unbearably long. It leads to womanising, idleness and other vices.

Unwittingly, just before independence the colonial authorities may have abetted more recent generations of elders in manipulating this waiting game. In 1960, for example, the administration ordered the tribe to bring the circumcision ceremony forward two years. Fourteen years later the new initiates were agitating for their circumcision but the elders remained unmoved – with good reason. Strategically it gave them another two years in which to take their pick of the young girls. The warriors waiting to move into elderhood were left to their idle ways.

THE SAMBURU do not regard sexual promiscuity as immoral. On the contrary, to keep young men in place the elders encourage them to take mistresses. But such relationships, however loving, can only be temporary. Nearly always the girl comes from the same clan and custom prohibits the couple marrying. If she does not come from the same clan, the warrior is often humiliated by an elder arbitrarily taking his mistress as bride.

The humiliation is real: Samburu men are affectionate and gentle with their women and tolerant enough to allow them discreet love affairs with men of their own age-set. The custom has some charm. It is notified to the husband by the spear the agemate leaves planted in the ground outside the marriage home. This is a sign that the warrior's wife is 'temporarily engaged', rather like a 'Do Not Disturb' notice on a hotel room door.

The seduction is elegant. The man will lie unmoving on the crude bed, his arms by his side, talking in poetic Samburu of romance until, overcome by his lyricism, the wife can no longer resist being unfaithful.

The husband's tolerance endures only until the wife becomes pregnant. Thereafter she is allowed no other lover and even sexual intercourse with her husband ceases until a year or more after she has given birth.

Children provide the couple with stability. They are a focus of interest and attention. However warriors have to wait a long time to achieve this stability – their time as bachelors lasts at least ten years.

The Samburu's age-set system, intricately spaced and designed to perpetuate the elitism of the elders, has therefore developed a number of mechanisms for controlling wayward warriors. When they become too sullen they are brought nearer the tribe. When they become too proud the tribe remains aloof and keeps them at a distance.

This delicate balancing act is performed around the ceremonies which begin with circumcision. Each ceremony is known as an *ilmugit* and at each the initiate is in close contact with his sponsor, the Samburu version of a Christian godfather.

These sponsors are junior elders one stage below the initiates' fathers. They have a name which describes their major duty – 'Firestick Elders'. When the date of the circumcision ceremony is named they kindle a fire to announce the spiritual birth of their 'godson' and his readiness to undergo circumcision. They have an extraordinary influence over the initiate throughout his life.

Each time there is an *ilmugit* the clan builds a settlement, the huts revolving in a clockwise circle in order of the seniority of the families. At every opportunity the firestick elders hector their charges on their responsibilities. The elders have the power to call special commissions or tribunals at which they can make specific charges of delinquency, or of defiance of the clan. This is about as close as Samburu culture comes to a judicial structure. It is perhaps no surprise that in a dispute the elders of two clans will stand against the warriors of one clan – by so doing they preserve the seniors' authority.

The Samburu lack any kind of formal political or ritual rule: instead authority is invested in the clan and the age-set system. So, though kinship binds the members of each clan closely to one another, there is often friction between different clans.

But, throughout, the elders use the *ilmugit* to perpetuate their authority. All young warriors know, too, that one day they will become elders with all the privileges inherent in this status. Thus silently they are complicit – they know that if they do not upset the system they will benefit from it in the end.

OF ALL their elaborate ceremonies, none is more intricate than the initiation into manhood involving circumcision followed three days later by a ritual hunt.

The Samburu boy before initiation belongs to the tribe's youngest age-set – one of the groups by which Samburu society measures the maturity of each generation. The wisest is the group of senior elders who traditionally control the circumcision ceremony, a mass ritual spaced at intervals which occur about every fourteen years.

The cut takes a minute. The initiation lasts a month. As soon as the circumciser finishes, the boy is carried inside his house to rest. A cocktail of curdled cow's milk and blood serves as a tonic. Later his father's agemates come to bless him, anointing his head with fat or butter.

This is an acknowledgement that he is ready to leave home. Armed with bow and arrows he goes to the forest and bush for a month. The purpose of this is to test his ability to live like his forebears among the wild animals of Africa.

Yet it is not a wild animal which the young man must bring down as proof of his qualities. Instead it is a small bird. The arrows he uses to do this are blunt, the rounded head of each one tipped with gum from the *silalei* tree.

Success renders a splendid, undamaged, natural specimen which is used as warrior ornamentation – each bird set into a head-dress testifies to the wearer's prowess.

When the month is up the initiate throws the head-dress away. Sometimes it is caught by coy girls, adroitly hiding, who prize this symbol of manhood.

The birds are not the initiate's only preoccupation. He is forbidden to wash, to sit on stones, or to use his hands to eat. The flesh of pig, game, fowl or bird are not to be tasted – only mutton. And honour, of course, is everything.

The late Joy Adamson in *Peoples of Kenya* observed something of the initiates' bravado when a group disturbed her in a forest glade. 'We had great fun together while I painted them,' she recalled. 'They boasted that one of their tests of courage was fixing a sandal onto a rhino's horn'.

This extravagant behaviour, steeped in binding traditions, is a unique expression of ethnic identity. It proclaims each individual a Samburu tribesman.

The proclamation is given shape in the form of a great feast after the initiates return home. For each initiate an ox is slaughtered and roasted. The young man takes his beast's thigh bone cleaving it in two with one blow of his wood club as token of his vow that no married woman will see him eat meat until he is welcomed into the ranks of the elders many years later. By such performances are Samburu youths elevated to exalted warrior status.

JOHN HILLABY described his first view of Samburu country at the beginning of Kenya's independence as 'looking over the edge of the world' from the top of a mountain.

'The frontier plains stretched out towards Ethiopia, a boundless expanse of sand and lava dust, broken only by the wrecks of ancient volcanoes, some with exquisite breast-like cones, straight-sided and nippled with rosettes of magma;

others had been worn down by the wind until, like the flat backs of a school of whales, they seemed to be swimming away, line astern, across a sea of sand.'

This erosion appalled Hillaby. He thought pastoralism was an 'expansive means of livelihood and the last resort of a doomed race'. More recent studies acknowledge that pastoralists like the Maasai and Samburu know a good deal more about the viable management of their environment than Hillaby realised.

The problem now is not one of pastoralism *per se*, nor of mismanagement, but of the growth of human and cattle populations. Health facilities for the people and veterinary medicine for the herds have created a new problem for the Samburu, a strange one: overcrowding.

The population explosion has wrought change in the all-important age-sets and clans. In the 1960s and 1970s some clans spread out beyond their traditional districts. There are signs that clan structures generally are drifting towards the more amorphous patterns already assumed by the larger Maasai tribe.

Even greater change is likely for the Samburu. The Kenya Government emphasises social welfare and basic education, and promotes an ethic of nationalism instead of tribalism. It is therefore safe to predict that the sectarian and segregationist philosophy which gave the tribe its special character when it walked out on its Maasai brothers more than two centuries ago will soon vanish.

Right: A young Samburu warrior leads his herd
along a track near Laisamis. Only those Samburu
in the drier regions close to the Ariaal Rendille
and the Rendille proper tend camels.

Previous pages: In what may well be one of the last circumcision ceremonies to be held by the Samburu tribe, black-robed initiates return from Lake Kisima after collecting water for blessing.

Left: The initiates have worn charcoal-blackened robes for the last month together with special ear ornaments. As the time for the ceremony nears they gather in the *Lorora* – the clan settlement specially built for the occasion on the slopes of the 6,000 foot Lorogi Plateau.

Below: Gathered together in the chill evening air the initiates bolster their courage by chanting the *lebarta* – a song which is said to be a particularly powerful form of coercion.

Prior to the circumcision ceremony an initiate's head is shaved by his mother (left). Reeds at the boy's elbow, and clay daubs on his cheeks, are proof that he made the twenty-four mile journey to Lake Kisima. Bottom left: elders prepare special sandals for the young initiates. After putting the sandals on (bottom right), each initiate will drive his family's cattle into the yard and then present himself for circumcision (opposite). Symbolically he spends his last moments as a youth sheltering beneath his mother's apron (overleaf, top left). Then, drenched in milk as a form of blessing (overleaf, bottom left), he steps forward naked. He sits down on a sheepskin rug in front of his mother's house where he is held by one man at his back and another at his right leg (overleaf, right). They become his ritual patrons. The skin at the end of the prepuce is cut off so the penis is completely free of it. Then a small hole about half an inch long is cut into the top of the prepuce and the penis is drawn through it. The circumciser trims the prepuce as it hangs down. The entire operation lasts about a minute, during which the initiate must not move or show pain.

Top left: After the operation the initiate sings *lebarta* and is promised a heifer by his father.

Bottom left: He is carried into his mother's hut and laid on a couch to rest.

Warriors secure a cow, subduing
it by spitting in its eye, tying
a thong around its neck and shooting
an arrow into its jugular. The frothing
blood pumps into a leather gourd to be
mixed with milk and is served to the
initiate as a recuperative tonic.

Above and left: One of the fledgling warrior's tests of skill during the month in the bush which follows his circumcision is to shoot small birds with an arrowhead which has been rounded with resin from a forest tree. Undamaged birds killed in this way are woven into a head-dress with ostrich feathers. Possession of such a head-dress attests to hunting prowess.

Opposite: The black robe distinguishes the initiate from the full-blooded warrior at left.

Above: The initiates' return from the bush is marked by a great feast at which an ox is butchered for each initiate to mark his elevation to the status of junior warrior.

Right: The initiates' oxen are grilled on open barbecue pits which are dug in a forest clearing and arranged in a circle which is exactly similar to the order in which the huts in the settlement are placed.

Above: During the feast, each initiate must crack the thigh bone of his ox with a single blow of his wood club, a token of his vow that no married woman will see him eat meat until he enters the ranks of the elders many years later.

Right: The feast marks a new relationship between the initiate and the two warriors who have been chosen to help him. Fat from the underside of the beast – *nkiyu* – is daubed on to the initiate, who is wearing strips of lion hide on his knees to signify the importance of the ceremony. From now on the three have reciprocal powers exactly the same as bond brothers.

Marriage is a joyful yet solemn
occasion for the polygamous Samburu.
They cherish and esteem their women
even though discreet affairs with
members of their own age-set are
tolerated. A groom watches happily in
the bridal hut as his bride is arrayed in
fine ornaments on the morning after
undergoing female circumcision. This
is only carried out when she has
become betrothed. Her arms are
decorated with a coil of brass.

Left: The groom and best man lead the
bride from her father's homestead as
the elders of all the clans bless them.

Below: The happy couple in their
wedding finery.

Samburu warriors (right) display their physique and fitness in a standing-jumping form of dance. Attractive young Samburu girls (below) dance among themselves. The coquettish young women are allowed to become mistresses of the warriors but are forbidden to marry them and must avoid pregnancy.

Left: Elegant decorations of a typical Samburu warrior.

Above: This Samburu warrior displays ear-rings of bones, and special facial markings.

Above right: No longer a warrior, this Samburu elder has shaved his head and wears little in the way of decorations. His status, like that of his colleagues, is judged by cattle, wives and children.

Right: Samburu warriors in the vivid finery of their rank: brightly coloured cloth, beaded necklaces, long hair, and fierce spears.

Overleaf: A mountain plateau in Samburu countryside.

TURKANA

The Savage Nobles

TO THE WEST OF LAKE TURKANA LIES A LARGE DESERT PUNCTUATED by a few mountains and one road. The only growing things are thorn bushes, their roots radiating as far as seventy feet afield for moisture, an occasional baobab, some heat-and-dust-loving succulents and desert grass.

This is the home of the 210,000-strong Turkana tribe. To them it is a cherished land. For centuries they have attacked their neighbours and, more recently, Britain's imperial forces, to keep what they have of it and to take more.

Manhood comes early and simply in such circumstances. The Turkana youth, aged between 16 and 20, must kill an ox in front of his elders. The spear he uses in the initiation ceremony must not pass through the beast. That would be a bad omen.

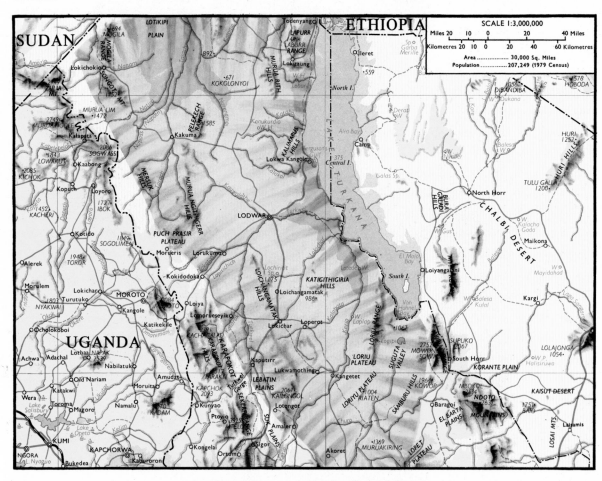

Previous page: A wrist knife and finger
knife are as much part of the Turkana elder's dress
as the oval-shaped tin nose ring.

The man becomes a warrior when he kills his first human enemy. He is given the name of the place where he took life so that no one will forget he is a warrior.

He is armed from the day of his initiation. His sponsor gives him a spear, other weapons, a stool which also serves as a head-rest, and a pair of sandals. In future these will carry him across sand and rock in search of enemies to raid, and land and livestock to steal.

He may go far. The Turkana district covers 30,000 square miles and is parcelled out into nineteen different territories populated by twenty-eight clans. The Turkana prize individualism and thus their society is loose-knit and ill-defined.

This emphasis on the individual shows up in a general disregard for the clan, the main function of which is to regulate weddings to ensure that each member of one clan marries into another. For the rest, the Turkana are indifferent to society. Indeed, clansmen are only one degree removed from strangers.

Another characteristic of the Turkana is that they have only the vaguest notion of their own history. The Turkana warrior is concerned predominantly with the present. More specifically, he focuses on two objectives: land and how to win it; livestock and how to acquire it.

The Turkana have pursued these twin aims with single-minded purpose for the last 300 years – from the time when the tribe broke away from the Karamajong-Teso plains Nilotes who had migrated south perhaps a thousand years before that. The new group settled in the semi-desert which stretches from Kapedo in the south to Sudan in the north, bounded in the west by Uganda and the Karapokot escarpment, and in the east by Lake Turkana, Mount Nyiru and the Lorogi Plateau.

These badlands have few resources. Progress and change are slow. In such territory nothing moves quickly except the nomad and his herds. Turkana district has fewer than twenty primary schools and only three secondary schools.

Tending five species of livestock – cattle, camels, sheep, goats and donkeys – the constant need of the Turkana is for grass and water. Neighbours are always temporary. As pastures diminish and wither, men go their own way. This state of affairs gives each man valuable flexibility, allowing him to decide his own destiny, moving his settlement according to climate, vegetation and, of course, his own temperament.

Approximately once every few decades the Turkana face the threat of extinction as drought seizes their rangelands. Famines come and go, taking lives with them. Thousands died in the 1920s and thousands in the 1960s. Thousands died again at the beginning of the 1980s.

Yet, out of this recurring hardship has been forged a fierce happiness. Born solely, it seems, to fight, the Turkana paradoxically are at peace with themselves. 'As a people,' says Alistair Graham, 'they are tough, wild and aggressive. At the same time they are peaceful in a way that only contented people can be. Turkana warriors will fight fiercely to the death and cherish the fighter's vocation above all else; yet they are devoid of viciousness or hatred. They are in equilibrium with their environment . . . One hears more laughter in the hard, harsh land of Turkana than anywhere else I know'.

There seems to be no particular reason for this Turkana enthusiasm for life. Their environment appals most outsiders – for example, a young British army officer posted there in 1917. 'To me,' wrote T. R. Cambridge in *In The Land of Turkana*, 'it appeared an arid, swelteringly hot, uncivilised, uncultivated, waterless, dried-up corner of the world.' Similarly, von Hohnel was unable to understand 'on what all the animals lived'.

Precisely because of this paucity of natural resources, the Turkana have become exceptionally thrifty. Nothing goes to waste. Having eaten all the lions in the region, they have started poaching Lake Turkana's crocodile. 'They eat everything,' von Hohnel observed, 'even their dogs, of which they have a good many.'

Crops are limited but Turkana value the worth of whatever they can induce to grow. They cultivate whenever the rains fall. Recently they have supplemented their meagre resources with fish – though their initial, exploratory techniques were clumsy and lacklustre: evidence of pastoral apathy towards this kind of food.

Willock once watched an old man paddling in the shallows of Lake Turkana with reed-torch and openwork basket which he dipped down at intervals occasionally coming up with a small tilapia. 'Here,' he wrote, 'is a method of fishing linking modern man with his stone-age ancestors'.

Graham observed another standing at the water's edge throwing a spear into the lake and retrieving the weapon by means of a rope tied to its end. 'He simply assumed that one day a fish would swim by at the instant his spear dove in, to be impaled on the inevitability of its own destiny ... It seemed to me that he had refined the art of fishing down to its essential elements and I could think of no better method to suggest to him'.

The Norwegian Government's overseas aid programme could think of better methods, and did. More than 3,000 Turkana now belong to the fishermen's co-operative based at Kalokol. They use dug-out canoes and fibreglass dinghies. The money they make seems to have overcome pastoralist disgust at the idea of fishing and fish-eating.

But still, the Turkana way of life is not centred on the business of fishing. War and cattle are the key. In this context, and particularly the latter, modernisation has produced a dangerous paradox. National policies have restricted the boundaries of the Turkana domain. Veterinary medicine has increased the size and improved the health of the Turkana herds.

Suddenly, the traditional equation has been inverted. Stock has become plentiful and grazing scarce. Inevitably this state of affairs has sharpened the edge of the Turkana's well-known hunger for land.

In the past warriors simply marched out and took land when they wanted it. Their expansionism was voracious. Land – any land, anywhere – was the sole aim. Early in this century such annexation was having a rebound effect on other tribes like the Pokot who found themselves forced into areas settled by white farmers.

The Pokot were not the only tribe affected. On one occasion in 1912 a band of cocky Turkana warriors trekked down the Rift to tackle the Maasai. The Turkana did not stay on the land but they did make off with 700 Maasai cattle.

To stand still in Turkana is to wither under the sun whereas to move forward is to seek new pasture, new hope, and new territory. This attitude was evidenced by the 1979 census which revealed remarkably little growth in the tribe's numbers. 'Many have moved out,' said a Kenya Government statistician. 'They have gone to Uganda and Sudan. Turkana people never stay long in one place.'

AT THE far south end of the Turkana's inhospitable land lies a natural oven where temperatures regularly touch 140 degrees Fahrenheit. This oven is enclosed on one side by the 4,000-foot Loriu Plateau, an almost impenetrable wedge of volcanic rock, cliffs, ravines and precipices. To the north, the oven is separated from Lake Turkana by the 3,500-foot mass of the Kangolenyang Mountains. Part of this mass is called The Barrier. The oven is the Suguta valley.

The Loriu Plateau has become a hideout for latter generations of Turkana warriors unable or unwilling to give up the ways of their forefathers. They are called *Ngorokos*, meaning outlaws. They have all the tools needed for mayhem and murder.

The Turkana's formidable arsenal of hand-to-hand weapons consists of spears and shields, fighting sticks and wood clubs, razor-sharp wrist and finger knives and long, thin needles on which to skewer the opposition.

Not entirely blind to the technology which in other ways they staunchly resist, the Turkana have supplemented these traditional weapons with stolen rifles. 'Among men for whom violence is still functional and honourable,' recorded Graham, 'our guns were professionally admired as fine weapons.'

The hand-to-hand weapons, still very much in use around the Loriu Plateau today, are fashioned by the tribe's smiths who hold a privileged position. They used to smelt their own ore but today work with scrap metal imported from outside the district.

The Turkana warrior's dress is little enough – just a loose cloth sometimes – but without his weapons he would feel naked. By carrying and using his weapons he earns the right to scarify his body: cicatrices on the upper right arm and chest denote male victims; on the left, female victims. There is no limit to the number of cuts made to denote each victim. A warrior also has the right to wear white ostrich feathers.

The warlike philosophy of the Turkana fascinated E. R. Shackleton, who was a District Commissioner in Lodwar during the 1930s. Shackleton recorded a long story told by a veteran chief named Lonyamon: 'I was a warrior. I knew everything. And ever since I have killed a man I have worn nothing but the best ostrich feathers – white'.

Lonyamon was explaining his sadness at a lost battle. 'And then my group was wiped out by the Merille. That defeated me. It still defeats me. Everything since that day has defeated me'.

'Timid people would be anything but comfortable in Turkana,' von Hohnel observed. 'They have triumphed over all their neighbours and stand in awe of none. Fortunately we were not troubled with nerves and therefore the wild goings on in camp did not affect us much. Now some warriors would dash down upon us as if to make a hostile charge and then there would be no end of noise and confusion over the purchase of some goats, the loud 'he he' of the natives resounding through the camp as if a fight were imminent'.

It was typical behaviour. Confronted with strangers the Turkana either attempt to intimidate them or else pretend indifference. 'They make you feel not just insignificant,' recorded Graham, 'but downright redundant'.

The first Turkana Hillaby encountered left the same impression. 'If they were surprised to see us, they kept their feelings to themselves . . . they looked up but said nothing and went on with their work.' It was proof enough of von Hohnel's statement. 'There are no half measures in the Turkana demeanour. Indecision and feebleness are rarely seen'.

In its long history of colonial conquest rarely did Britain find more determined adversaries. The Turkana provoked either admiration or contempt among early administrators.

'The Turkana,' reported one, 'were the finest fighting men in East Africa'.

'The Turkana,' said another, 'are undoubtedly the lowest type of native in East Africa'.

'From their first contact with Europeans,' wrote James Barber in *Imperial Frontier*, 'they had revealed an aggressive attitude, a refusal to accept lightly interference or control. This bred respect as well as hostility from British officials'.

Major Harry Rayne found that the Turkana prided themselves on their fierceness, blood-thirstiness and treachery.

Time has done nothing to diminish Turkana arrogance or sartorial style. Adorned only with his head-dress, and ivory plugs under his lower lip, plaited leather on his arms and legs, the Turkana warrior somehow evokes an image of a naked Roman Centurion. It is a just comparison. The Turkana have all the qualities which would have won them honour in ancient Rome.

Striding through the desert with the loping gait characteristic of the African nomad, these warriors form an unforgettable vision. Their striking appearance and physique, and qualities of courage and endurance, have left a vivid impression on many people including Cambridge. 'The Turkana are a brave tribe,' he wrote, 'and would make remarkably good soldiers'.

But Turkana military aptitude was no unrealised potential. It was a convincing reality as the British were to discover.

TWO FACTORS precipitated the British presence in Turkana land: the tribe's expansionism and the baroque ambitions of Emperor Menelik II of Abyssinia, now the modern state of Ethiopia.

As early as the 1890s Menelik's agents had armed some tribesmen and had also staked out claims which were to persist well into the twentieth century. Menelik claimed the territory north of the Turkwel river. He even installed a 'Governor' at Maji in the country's southern province of Kaffa.

At that time British-ruled Uganda was not interested in the southern half of Turkana land, which had been designated as its Rudolf Province. The civil service at Entebbe simply saw no profit in this unproductive wilderness. The British in what was to become the colony of Kenya were interested however, and it was to cost them dear.

What the British did not, and possibly could not, foresee was the expense in arms, ammunition and men required to take over Turkana territory. The tribe preferred to die rather than to concede.

The British aim was nothing short of total subjugation. An official report flatly defined the policy as 'the gradual conquest of the Turkana'. This 'gradual conquest' became a violent enterprise to subdue a properly drilled, armed and determined people.

Britain's presence in Turkana was first established in 1905–06. During that period the Baringo District Commissioner followed the length of the Kerio River from its source on 9,000-foot Kapkut mountain, near Timboroa on the Equator, to its mouth on the lake. The military followed. In 1910, troops of the King's African Rifles marched into the area and seized 16,000 head of Turkana stock calling this action compensation and punishment.

Seizing stock was the British way of impressing Crown authority on the Turkana, but the tribe interpreted such behaviour differently – as rustling on a massive scale. They saw no reason to acquiesce. From defence they sprang to attack.

At any one time the well-drilled Turkana could put 25,000 warriors into the field, and they were masters of desert warfare. 'Their intimate knowledge of the country,' wrote Barber, 'and their ability to survive in the toughest conditions, made them flexible and quick in their movements.' The British, by contrast, must have appeared slow and cumbersome. They could not operate far from major water points; food had to be carried with them wherever they marched.

The logistics were overwhelming. Cambridge's journey gives some idea of the immense task involved in moving troops into Turkana. He travelled by rail from Nairobi to Kisumu, by steamer across Lake Victoria to Entebbe to return along the north shore to Jinja; thence he went by rail to Lake Kioga, by steamer to Lale and by foot to Moroto on the Karamoja escarpment overlooking Turkana. All this took one man several weeks: consider, therefore, the task of moving hundreds or thousands of troops across such terrain.

By 1915 Turkana firepower amounted to more than 2,000 rifles. That was also the year in which the tribe lost at least 400 warriors and 19,000 cattle, 215 camels, 1,400 donkeys, and 17,000 head of small stock. The British gave them back a third of the animals. The Turkana made up most of the rest of their loss violently, at the expense of their neighbours.

As a result the British organised a punitive expedition of 710 soldiers led by British officers. Many of the African askaris objected and mutinied. They were disarmed by their officers and sent back to Nairobi in disgrace. The rest slaughtered Turkana women and children.

THE PUNITIVE expeditions organised by the British over a number of years succeeded to some extent in keeping the Turkana down. But by no means could they ever have been called 'a conquest'. Pax Britannica, in other words, may have rendered the tribe incapable of major war but it never left them completely impotent. The policy of containment was to rebound on the British anyway. The problem was that the Turkana's traditional enemies were not policed with the same ruthlessness as the Turkana themselves. By the early 1920s the Turkana, to all intents, were disarmed. This upset the traditional balance of power in the region. As an official report compiled many years later conceded, British policy put the Turkana at the mercy of the 'Abyssinia ruffians' and the Merille and Donyiro.

Undisputed masters of this arid region from time immemorial, the Turkana suddenly found themselves faced by superior numbers and superior weapons, and were now to suffer the fury of an exultant Merille eager to pay off scores which stretched back centuries.

The Merille killed unknown hundreds of Turkana in a series of raids in 1924. Later, in April 1927, they slaughtered 80 fishermen. The massacres continued until September 1933 when a period of uneasy peace began. But in 1939 the Merille, armed by the Italian conquest of Abyssinia and trained by Mussolini's forces in guerilla warfare, killed almost 300 Turkana in one raid.

'It was not easy to protect the Turkana,' noted the British, 'since raiders could not be pursued across the border.'

Accordingly, as Turkana suffering grew, the British relented. The proposal to rearm the Turkana had often been made but never acted upon. Finally, when Britain went to war with Italy in Africa in June 1940 the Turkana were rearmed. Within months, the Merille were chased well back into Ethiopia, suffering heavy losses at the hands of the Turkana's refurbished warriors.

TURKANA QUALITIES are not just heroic. As a people they mellow with long acquaintance. Those who spend time with them often come to see them not only as bloody-minded individuals but as shrewd, likeable, companionable and highly intelligent.

The Turkana have a remarkable language; it includes 23 verbs simply to describe a person's walk. This makes them highly articulate, by any measure, and certainly far removed from von Hohnel's picture of 'grotesque dances, noisy unmelodious songs, wild ungainly jumping accompanied by obscene gestures and a long drawn howl of 'hu hu hu'.'

They are superstitious and inclined to invoke supernatural forces to explain anything they do not understand. Teleki, on his arrival amongst the Turkana, was at once summoned to make rain – why else would a person of such strange colour have been sent to them?

Turkana are also deeply suspicious by nature – of all things and all men. One family was so incensed by the questions of a visiting anthropologist they packed up home, marched out their cattle and disappeared in the middle of the night leaving him to wake in surprised solitude. Questions, cameras and notebooks are anathema.

Many Turkana read the future by tossing their sandals in the air and observing the way they fall. Larger mysteries are solved by the witchdoctors who throw old bones to study future portents. In the region in general, all this is regarded as powerful magic. The Rendille and Samburu are so convinced of the effects of Turkana witchcraft they put their finger in a Turkana footprint and place it on their forehead to remove any possible curse.

Turkana culture also yields a store of artefacts which can justifiably be judged art: among them are elaborate beaded necklaces for the women and elegant hand-carved stools on which warriors may sit or rest their heads.

The homes of the Turkana are scraps of thorn branches, woven with leaves and skins into the shape of a geodesic dome – the traditional design of these areas. Perhaps this domestic simplicity helps to sum up a people who ask for little except land and cattle. They have what Graham believes is a peculiarly nomadic cultural attribute – a sense of equilibrium. He defines it as harmony, stability and contentment, 'qualities urban man finds increasingly elusive'.

So too, it has to be said, does the Turkana nomad of today. His traditions are being disturbed by the need for Kenya to mould a cohesive, progressive nation founded on a modern industrial base. The new factory at Kalokol has served notice on the Turkana warrior that his time is running out.

The problem is that anything less than life as a warrior is beneath him. Alone among the renowned fighting tribes of East and Central Africa, the Turkana still cling tenaciously to their heritage of deadly strife – as anachronistic as their belief that the world is flat. If not the noble savages of romantic writers, they certainly warrant the title of savage nobles – a unique aristocracy now, like the American Indian a century ago, in conflict with a foe they can neither understand nor defeat.

Previous pages: The Turkana scrape a living in a land of sweltering heat using donkeys as pack beasts across their rocky 30,000 square mile domain.

Left: Water is a scarce and precious commodity mostly found in holes dug in dried-up river beds. Here a young child draws rations for the family. Even Turkana cattle have learned to dig their way down to water with their hooves.

Below: A young girl carries home water in a wooden, hand-carved vessel. Green fronds floating in the water help prevent spillage.

Far left: Turkana women are extremely fond of dancing, the normal style of which consists of a simple jumping motion. They wear little in the way of clothes but collect an abundance of necklaces, sometimes as many as fifty. A single plain metal circle is given to a bride upon payment of the dowry and denotes that she is married.

Above: Hours are spent in creating elaborate coiffeurs by braiding and shaving the hair.

Left: A Turkana beauty with an extravagance of necklaces, some of them made from the potent black seed *enus* which serve as a decoration, others from the root *ekeriau* which serves as protection against man and beast. Its aroma is reputed to ward off danger, and extra potency is achieved by the wearer chewing a small piece and spitting it out at intervals.

The Turkana are traditionally nomadic pastoralists but recurring famine has driven increasing numbers to fishing. Now a co-operative has attracted thousands as full-time fishermen. Nile perch such as these (left) bring rich rewards at the Kalokol market. Indeed, so good is the living to be made that within a decade fishing has become the single most important industry around Turkana and many new villages have sprung up. Their sun-dried catches (below) are sold at lakeside markets and shipped to Kalokol.

Opposite: Assembled in their finery, these Turkana elders display the demeanour of honoured warriors with ostrich feathers for headgear and an arsenal of wrist and finger knives.

Above: Fearless warriors and hunters, Turkana men are invested with a natural grace and dignity. In his finery of leopard skin and ostrich feathers, a venerable chief poses outside his home with some of his wives.

Left: All Turkana men carry small wooden stools with them wherever they go. The stools double up as pillows.

Overleaf: Shadowed by the bulking heights of the Lapurr Range, a young Turkana goatherd tends his flock.

MERILLE

The Nameless Nomads

IF THEY WERE NOT MEMBERS OF ONE OF AFRICA'S MOST RUTHLESS
tribes the men who live on the banks of the River Omo, second only in size among
Ethiopian rivers to the Blue Nile, might be regarded as transvestites.

When a Merille is initiated as a man he pretends to be a woman. Circumcision
takes place late, sometimes in his late twenties or early thirties. It is not difficult to
identify the initiate. He spends his convalescence wearing skirts and women's
ornaments and he is treated as if he were a nursing mother.

Nothing in their history explains this custom but what history is available is
scant and ill-recorded. The first Westerners to contact the tribe – in April, 1888 –
were, once again, the indomitable Count Teleki and his friend von Hohnel. This

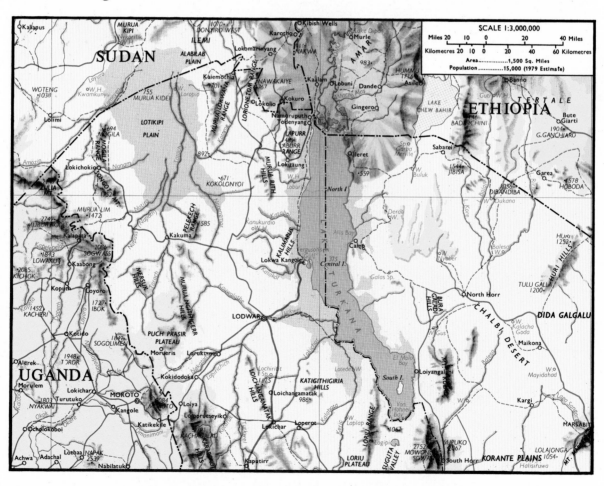

Previous page: Merille elders practise elaborate weaving
of the hair. Metal ear-rings are much favoured,
however little other ornamentation is worn.

first encounter with Europeans was almost certainly the first time the Merille had seen a rifle. They were impressed with the 'firesticks' because they had the capacity to kill swiftly, from a distance. For a people apprenticed in war from childhood the rifle was at once an object of beauty. And today it is still a weapon which the Merille cherish. Indeed it is one of the few indications that they have had any contact with external civilisation.

The Merille call themselves *Dassenech*. Teleki used yet another name for them, *Reshiat*. They also use the names *Gelubba* and *Shangilla*. But, call them what you will, they are a case-book study of an untrammelled people living almost exactly now as they have done for centuries.

The Merille's present territory is set in a kidney-shaped 1,500-square miles of semi-desert which embraces Teleki's Lake Stefanie, now called *Chew Bahir*, and the north-west, north and north-east shores of Lake Turkana. It is here that the River Omo decants itself into Lake Turkana.

'We stood,' recounted von Hohnel, 'upon the threshold of northern Gallaland in the district belonging to Reshiat or Rissiat who occupy the northern shores of Lake Rudolf, which is here fringed with reeds and rushes, whilst beyond stretches a flat tract of country overgrown by an impenetrable forest from which rises but one mountain mass, the five-peaked Mount Nakua, whilst far away in the distance the horizon is shut out by a chain of heights varying in altitude from about 1,640 to 3,280 feet'.

The impenetrable forest and the reeds and rushes have had their effect – the etymology and geography of this part of Lake Turkana remains incomplete.

Even the Merille's national identity is doubtful. They spill into Kenya on both sides of the lake – at Ileret and between Lokitaung and Namuruputh. They have little respect for frontier posts. They do not carry passports for, like other pastoralists, they are indifferent to bureaucracy.

They also have a reputation for being unimpressed by strangers. 'The way in which these natives,' recounted von Hohnel, 'who had hitherto lived quietly far away from the rest of the world, received us on this first day of our arrival was so simple, so utterly unlike anything related in the accounts of their experiences by African travellers, that we could not get over our astonishment'. Even before, when Teleki's advance party made up of Africans had come upon the tribe, von Hohnel found that their stoicism and impassivity had made a great impression on the expedition's head man. 'He thought they must be a very powerful tribe if the sudden appearance of 40 men who might have dropped from the skies affected them so little'.

It takes more than strangers to interfere with the Merille warriors' favourite relaxation of sitting. All men carry a stool which, at intervals, they will plonk down at what to them seems a congenial spot in what, to anyone else, is an undistinguished desert. 'The older men set very little store on weapons, dress or ornament,' notes von Hohnel, 'but they always carry in the right hand the indispensable *karro*, which serves as seat, bolster, and sometimes also as tobacco pouch. No male Reshiat is ever seen without his *karro*, but women do not use them at all'.

Merille men much prefer sitting around to getting on with the business of growing food. The land from which they scrape an existence is a rich alluvial basin periodically flooded by the Omo when the rains are good. This is the only time the Merille put away their stools and revert to cultivation.

In the 1960s they were taught the secret of irrigation by American missionaries who introduced a Cretan design of sail windmill. Lush gardens of melon, paw-paw, tomato, maize, sorghum and millet sprang up. Now the Americans have gone and the gardens have atrophied and returned to wilderness. One might cynically add, in the new Ethiopia, that instead of fruits the Merille today enjoy a diet of Marxist dialectic fed to them by Cuban 'agricultural advisers'.

It makes no difference. Nothing can replace the ideology of relaxation – as the gaunt rib-cages of the tribe's herds testify. Polemic has no influence amongst a people whose values are set solid on social and community prestige and cattle owning.

THE MERILLE are not a pure ethnic group. They have absorbed migrants and dissidents from other tribes. Some anthropologists feel that the tribal concept in the Merille context needs to be redefined – as a link based on the residential group rather than on heredity. At any rate, immigrants who come to live among the Merille, and who abide by their traditions and values, are accepted as Merille regardless of their ancestry or place of origin.

Many Turkana, Rendille and Samburu exiles today live as Merille as has traditionally been the case. 'Reshiat men,' wrote von Hohnel, 'prefer Samburu women as wives, they being ... distinguished from other negresses by their winning, self-possessed manners and their beautiful expressive eyes. The offspring of these unions are of a nobler type and they also seem to be more intelligent. We could always distinguish them by their eyes'.

The Merille are a mongrel tribe, in fact; but in terms of their values and traditions they are unique and therefore pure.

They are also amongst the least-known people of Africa. Even Ethiopia, which claims the majority of the Merille as its nationals, had only a passing knowledge of their existence until the turn of the century. At that time, Emperor Menelik's agents infiltrated the area and provided the tribe with arms and ammunition in the hope of using them as frontline troops to secure north Turkana for the Ethiopian flag.

It was not to be. At a 1907 meeting in Addis Ababa imperial boundaries were arbitrarily ruled on the map delineating territories and regions on which none of the delegates had set eyes, let alone foot. The thin red border lines of Sudan, Ethiopia and Kenya merged in Merille territory, creating the Ilemi Triangle, a valueless piece of real estate ostensibly owned by Sudan but policed by Kenya.

This fragmentation has since deprived Kenya of control of the lake's north shore, creating in the Delta a form of suzerainty which has confused the Merille. They are semi-nomadic, used to wandering freely between Kenya and Ethiopia. Today they find themselves increasingly constrained by border posts and entry formalities.

More than confusion, since the 1907 Anglo-Ethiopian accords a state of near-perpetual war has existed in the Ilemi Triangle between all the tribes – and between hostile national forces during the world wars.

Mussolini's presence – which resulted in the defeat of Abyssinia in 1937 – not only gave the Merille valuable lessons in guerilla warfare but also introduced a new source of weapons. More recent conflicts have continued to provide the Merille with a seemingly limitless stock of firepower to be incorporated into the tribal armoury at every opportunity. The lethal bric-à-brac of small arms left by the Uganda conflict in the late 1970s once again replenished Merille supplies of ammunition and weapons.

The tribe's prowess with guns is legendary and they use them with effect. The Merille are the scourge of the Gabbra and Rendille, raiding far down into Kenya. Their most implacable enemy, however, is the Turkana. The two cannot resist bickering even when restrained by effective policing. Like bad-tempered children constantly pulling each other's hair when teacher is not looking, neither loses the opportunity to provoke.

'The Merille,' wrote the late Joy Adamson, 'are truculent instigators of such fights and may kill the donkey of a passing Turkana out of pure mischief. The Turkana then retaliate and kill livestock belonging to the Merille. It is after such incidents, when blood is up on both sides, that murder is liable to take place'.

There is reason to be terrified of the Merille. If the Turkana notch their bodies to demonstrate the number of victims they have despatched, the Merille warriors have a more bizarre badge of valour. Traditionally, they castrate their victims and place the shorn genitalia around their own necks.

Hillaby reports one el-Molo's account of a Merille attack which came just before dawn, a time favoured by the tribe for such business. Hillaby's el-Molo informant claimed to have been woken by screams and to have fled with everybody else. 'When they crept back next morning a youth had disappeared. They found him by the edge of the lake still alive but mutilated. A young Merille must produce physical evidence of a successful raid before he can select a bride'.

Perhaps von Hohnel and Teleki were lucky to come upon the Merille in one of their quieter moments. Naively, the two Austrians considered a 'forcible solution' when the Merille refused to allow the expedition to continue through the tribal lands to cross the Omo and achieve a complete circumnavigation of Lake Rudolf. 'The Reshiat had received us kindly and dealt honourably with us; we did not want them to repent having done so, or to turn their first coming into contact with civilisation into a curse.' It might have been the Austrians who would have repented if battle had taken place.

In the end, however, it was not the Merille but the weather and lack of supplies which thwarted Teleki's grand design. Scouts surveyed the route but the rains had arrived. The Omo was in flood and the expedition had to retrace its steps back down the eastern shore.

IN MERILLE society, the most profound influence is the traditional age-class system. The clans have little inherent use. They function simply as a convenient way of absorbing new immigrants. Each new group forms a new clan and eventually a new section.

Absolute authority is exercised by a council of elders, thirty members of a senior age-class who wield extraordinary judicial and ceremonial powers. They are called the 'bulls' and they provide stud animals to Merille herdsmen for breeding purposes.

These elders are also the patrons of the tribe's annual *dimi* ceremony at which all first-born girls between seven and eight years old receive the council's blessings for their future fertility. The celebration is a six-week festival of dancing, food and wine. It emphasises the importance of the young girls who will raise the tribe's future generations but it is an expensive affair. The girls' fathers traditionally slaughter their entire herds, which leaves them impoverished.

The sacrificial act elevates the fathers to cherished elderhood. But the price of this status is the herds they have painstakingly developed since their marriage. It is one of many paradoxes in this society.

It is through marriage, first of all, that a Merille improves his social standing. Each man manipulates his land and animal holdings by using the new relationships which marriage has created. Since the dowry is paid in instalments over thirty years or more, the husband has ample opportunity to develop and exploit the ties within his wife's family. A whole range of options opens up with his in-laws creating the potential to gain prestige with other kinsmen and bond-partners by effectively influencing the distribution of the bride price.

In all this, the husband's father-in-law is a valuable oracle when it comes to deciding who gets what. Ideally, a man should end up with large herds, many wives and children – and the social prestige which goes with such assets. It does not always work out. As with any other society, the Merille have privileged, middle and poor classes.

But when the *dimi* signals the emergence of his daughter as a future mother the Merille man's animal holdings are liquidated anyway. Now he is entirely dependent on his family and relatives and in a subordinate position very similar to the lifelong status of the Merille woman who is allowed to own nothing from the day she is born.

This shadowy transvestism runs through the entire sequence of male life indicating a powerful spiritual respect for the woman's role. It is a curious paradox that men who can deftly emasculate their enemies in battle can also unashamedly indulge in rites which could mark them out as homosexuals in a more sophisticated society.

Each phase of manhood is symbolic of the woman's life cycle. For the Merille female the three major events in life are circumcision by clitoridectomy, between the ages of eight and ten, the *dimi* ceremony and the birth of her first child.

The men imitate this cycle. When they achieve puberty they undergo a ritual imitation of clitoridectomy and, some years later, a physical circumcision of the foreskin.

In no other society in Africa is the initiate treated with such care. He is pampered with exaggerated attention, his food specially prepared, his every need considered. The simile which anthropologist Uri Almagor draws is that of a nursing mother just after giving birth. Indeed, the parallels are so close that for weeks the newly-circumcised warrior wears a woman's skirts and ornaments.

All this helps to underscore the pertinence of woman in Merille society – owning nothing, deciding nothing, yet every aspect of her life foreshadows the rituals of manhood. It is perhaps not so out of place as it first seems that when you visit a Merille village you find it is the men who play with the children.

IT IS almost certain the Merille way of life will endure intact into the twenty-first century. Their resistance to change is passive where the Turkana's is violent. Somehow symbolic of this passivity is the fact that the American missionary windmills, which brought the lesson of year-round crops, were discarded as soon as the missionaries were expelled by the revolutionary Ethiopian government.

The Merille are a living microcosm of African society before the intrusion of Europe and the rest of the world. Their reaction to modern devices is pagan. Teleki and von Hohnel carried false teeth and glass eyes and beads to bewitch those they encountered.

Today's travellers, with rear-view mirrors on rarely seen cars and instant cameras, which develop a picture in a minute, produce the same expressions of innocent wonder among these isolated people.

They are a link with traditions and cultures which in almost every other part of the African continent have been overwhelmed and eroded by the pace of technological innovation.

Right: Gourds, buckets, old tins, donkeys –
all form part of the water corps and its equipment.
In Merille territory a day's water supply for a
family often lies many miles from home.

Above: Devastating flash floods occasionally roar through this dried-up river bed and then vanish almost as quickly as they came. Beneath the surface of the sand such floods leave behind a precious reserve of water for which the Merille families will dig deep.

Left: Leaves from acacias and desert succulents are placed in the water pans to prevent spillage.

Opposite: Miles from her settlement a young woman begins the long trek home with her precious load of water. She wears nothing but a leather skirt, neatly embroidered with a metal hem.

Above left: Fashion fancies still dominate the feminine soul even in far-away places like the Omo Delta. Here the vogue is leather skirts, embroidered at the hem with heavy metal ornaments.

Left: Reed mats, old skins, and some ancient hessian serve as home for most Merille families.

Above: Merille land offers little sustenance to man or beast except during the Omo floods. Water has to be carried long distances and children start this task early.

Left: Merille girls are often radiant beauties by their early teens.

Below: Smiling Merille maiden. Tribal custom decrees that from birth to death she will own nothing.

Above: Merille pastoral habits have reduced their grazing lands to a desolate waste which is matched by the paucity of their homes.

Right: A Merille stockman stands guard over his herd and practises with an old World War Two firearm. Rifles are common and most Merille men carry one.

The men spend much of their time sitting on elegant carved stools which also serve as pillows (opposite, top). A feather worn in the hair (opposite, bottom right) means that a man has killed and castrated an enemy. Despite the pursuit of prestige through battle, however, the Merille accumulate little in the way of lasting wealth. The Merille elder pictured (opposite, bottom left) wears a traditional ivory plug in his chin and a simple necklace – probably his sole possessions.

Following pages: Merille stockmen swim their herds across the Omo, fastening the beasts to dugout canoes.

As darkness comes the women turn for home.

GABBRA

The Desert Survivors

THE HOME OF THE GABBRA IS A LAND TO NUMB THE MIND. HARDLY A blade of grass peeps through the unproductive soil. The heat blinds and deadens the senses. Mirages shimmer on the horizon. Water is rare, and sometimes foul. The sun's rays have bleached the earth. If you walk through this area from Marsabit Mountain in the south, 200 miles to Sabarei on the Ethiopian border in the north, you will ask yourself how anything can survive.

Why do the Gabbra choose to live here?

Historically little is known about the tribe. Few strangers have spent any time in this part of the world. Of those who did – with the exception of Captain C. H. Stigand in 1910 – none stayed to ask about the people.

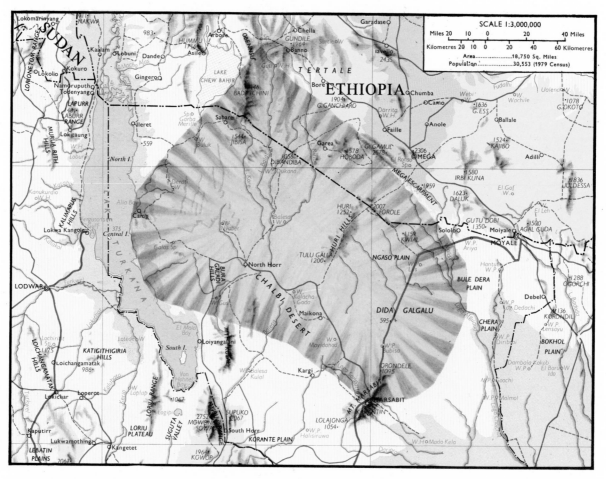

Previous page: A Gabbra elder.
Despite their peaceful nature, events of the last century
have taught the Gabbra to trust no-one.

124

Culturally the tribe is close to the Borana group from which they derive their name. Gabbra means "inferior", but clearly they are not.

Indeed with their distinctive features, fine eyebrows and high foreheads, skin oiled and glistening, many of these 30,000 people appear as patriarchs from an Old Testament lithograph.

They roam 18,750 square miles of harp-shaped wilderness. Ninety five per cent of this area is semi-arid or arid – between the west slopes of Ethiopia's Mega escarpment as far as Arbore on the north shore of *Chew Bahir*, Teleki's Lake Stefanie, and south through the Chalbi Desert and the Dida Galgalu plains to Marsabit.

The environment has produced a unique social structure forming a well-orchestrated, well coordinated, highly articulate pastoral community. Only so resilient a society could have overcome the threat of extinction that the Gabbra faced at the end of the nineteenth century.

The chronicle of disaster which the tribe endured began in 1887 when they were struck consecutively by rinderpest which destroyed their herds, malaria which decimated the population, smallpox, drought, internecine warfare and colonial conquest. These ordeals lasted until 1901.

THE GABBRA have only a few permanent watering-places for their mixed herds of camels, sheep, cattle and goats. The cattle fare better in the highland areas but there the camels are prone to tick-borne diseases.

The permanent watering-places are in the north-east of the Dida Galgalu plains and at the base of the Mega escarpment in Ethiopia. To the west is the Chalbi Desert, long ago part of the Lake Turkana basin, which sometimes suffers rare but devastating floods which turn it once again into a shimmering sheet of water. The rainfall, however, is not only rare but irregular. In sixty years there were only six wet seasons – 1916–17, 1934, 1937, 1954, 1958 and 1974.

When rain comes it restores the water table barely enough to allow the Gabbra herds to survive. The growth potential is too low to permit the grasses to recover. Scattered, minimal showers do occur each year for a period of up to three months but, by and large, forage in the land of the Gabbra is confined to standing hay, twigs and dried leaves from dwarf shrubs.

The perennial grasslands have their own constraints. Water is rare in the Huri Hills, on the Dida Galgalu Plains and at Arbore Jaban where the grass exists. The cattle can feed, but they cannot drink. And at the permanent watering places the land is so over-grazed there is nothing to eat. Fear of Merille and Rendille raids prohibits the use of pastures on Mount Kulal, while ticks and tsetse fly in other areas compound the Gabbra's problems.

Their technique is to fan out into the Chalbi and Kaisut Deserts when the rains begin, making use of shallow depressions and rock pools for water. When the rains end and the water diminishes, the herds move towards the permanent watering places.

This strategy inevitably strains the tribe's limited manpower resources. The herds are often spread out in four or five locations. As a consequence the Gabbra have developed a remarkable social unity. This unity is strikingly different from the ethics of other pastoral societies which call for independence and individuality.

Gabbra tribesmen start work at the age of seven and do not retire until they are old men. When the only guarantee of survival is co-operative labour everybody works, even the sick.

The need to survive also breeds stoicism, as Hillaby found out when he met a Gabbra youth near Alia Bay. 'He had been savaged by a lion ... I looked at the black crusted area of skin from which a portion the size of a fist had been torn out below the shoulder blade.' The attack had taken place a fortnight before. Hillaby wanted to know why the boy had not gone to the government health clinic at North Horr. 'But who will look after my goats?'

THE GABBRA are perhaps the closest-knit pastoral community in Africa. Families stay together to form cohesive, functional labour units.

Fathers and sons, particularly eldest sons who will eventually inherit their fathers' positions, are encouraged to live together even after the sons marry.

An essential component of bride price is the duty of the groom to live with his bride's family for a year. Often his father chooses to go with him. Indeed, in the land of the Gabbra, entire families – parents, sisters, married sisters, sons and married brothers – often live as one unit, sharing domestic duties and locking up their separate herds each night in the same kraal.

Marriage forms a lasting bond between the two families and the two clans. Each has a responsibility to help the other. The marriage ties outweigh the parochial loyalties of the tribe's different sections. Marriage ties mean pooled resources of labour and stock to fight the threats of drought and famine, disease and warfare.

Traditionally, the Gabbra despise trade. For the most part, they sell only when approached by neighbouring tribes or by Somali middle men. One neighbouring people are the Rendille with whom the Gabbra were once allied, sharing inheritances and stock, and even inter-marrying. But events were to set them apart from each other.

Today the Gabbra's only allies are the Galla Borana. They seem to be one and the same: their language and dress are common and two of the Gabbra's five sections claim descent from the Galla Borana. In fact, the two tribes have developed entirely different social structures, though they do still share a common distaste for trading which they consider beneath their dignity.

The Gabbra's only regular trading partner is the Konso tribe of Ethiopia whose smiths make the metal jewellery used in Gabbra rituals. These rituals are an important element of the community structure. The Gabbra have created offices akin to those of priest and high priest, and the special duties of the *High Xallu* are all connected with rituals. Judicial and other disputes are settled by the *Jallaba*. A group of political elders, the *Jallaba*, deals with most of the squabbles which might upset the tribe – arguments over watering rights and troubles between man and wife. They can impose fines and have the power to demand cattle for clan sacrifices. The *Jallaba* is also responsible for acting as a sectional – or tribal – council of war, organising raids.

But when a problem goes beyond the *Jallaba's* authority it is passed to the Gabbra's chief justice, the *Hayyu*, the most important and most coveted office in the tribe. The *Hayyu* deals only with extremely serious offences.

The political rulers who govern the tribe's homogeneous affairs demonstrate the validity of the argument for serving an apprenticeship in power. The Gabbra system ensures a gradual assumption of responsibility. The transition from one government to another is thus smooth.

The members of the incoming age-grade take over in co-operation with the members of the governing age-grade who are gently eased out of office to become holy men. Eventually they are edged out from this position too, to enjoy a comfortable retirement.

One of the tragedies underlying the tribe's recent history was the colonial administration's assumption that the age-grades posed a threat to peace. On the contrary, they are designed to maintain it. Based on a seven-year cycle, prone to interruption by natural disaster or war, they do not constitute a call-up system. They provide an organised hierarchical structure for law and order: the antithesis of what the bureaucracy thought.

UNTIL 1896 the Gabbra had little history of warfare. But that year both the British and Ethiopians sent scouts into the area.

The sight of Emperor Menelik's modern weapons was the tribe's first confrontation with military technology. The Emperor's herds had been hard hit by rinderpest and he had no compunction about using guns and bullets to acquire new, disease-free rangelands.

When the Imperial forces from Addis Ababa arrived the Gabbra took up their spears to march into battle and were mown down.

'From then on, Menelik's army took what it wanted,' said an old tribesman, 'when they said give, it was given. If it was not, they took by force.'

Seeking escape from this domination, and from a newly introduced tax system, the Gabbra fled south-west into the Chalbi Desert and on to the shores of Lake Turkana.

They were desperate. War had disturbed the balance of their struggle to survive. Rinderpest had decimated their stock. They took up arms and raided the Merille, stealing their cattle.

The Gabbra also went to their traditional allies and friends, the Konso, with whom for centuries they had traded sheep, goats, leather and salt for grain, cloth, iron, tobacco and coffee. They begged replacements for their herds. They approached the Somali. They were not traders but now they had no options. What could they give?

The Somali wanted elephant tusks and rhino horn. The Gabbra provided: two tusks bought thirty head of cattle and an equivalent number for rhino horn. It was at this point that the Gabbra became large-scale commercial hunters wiping out both species in their territory.

The Somali sought another commodity – women. Could the Gabbra provide it? They did. The price: one sack of grain for one virgin daughter. Even this desperate measure was excusable. It was the last throw of a people on the verge of extinction.

The raids on the Merille intensified the Gabbra's agony. The Merille were incensed and returned in force – banishing the Gabbra forever from their traditional grazing lands around Ileret. Well-watered, these were the best rangelands in Gabbra territory. The tribe sought new pastures and raided the Samburu.

News of the Gabbra's distress reached the Turkana, far away on the other side of the lake and they came raiding, scenting new trophies of land and livestock. A combined Borana-Gabbra army put to them to flight, however, and the Gabbra continued to occupy the land around North Horr unaware of the Pandora's Box they had opened.

When they did wake up to the danger it was too late. Suddenly, on all sides, the Gabbra were beset by enemies of their own making – and enemies they did not expect. In 1900, three years after their defeat, the Turkana returned in a classic demonstration of aggressiveness and military tactics, striking at nine targets in one swoop – selected watering-points in the Chalbi.

The Gabbra struck camp and made off towards Ethiopia only to be met by Menelik's men again. Desperate, the tribe turned south; but there they found the Samburu and the British. Wherever they went they were beset by enemies more powerful than themselves.

This pattern of decline was to continue. The Gabbra brought their own traditional alliance with the Rendille to an end by their assault on the Rendille's Samburu friends. Afterwards the beleaguered tribe withdrew into the wilderness it now occupies.

Then in the 1960s and 1970s the Somali *shifta*, raiding brigands from across the border between Kenya and the Somali Republic, linked up with the Rendille on one side and the Merille on the other. Gabbra stock losses were severe. In 1970 alone the Merille rode out with 5,000 head.

What made all this worse for the Gabbra was the tight control exercised within Kenya which was never reciprocated by the Somali or Ethiopian authorities.

The Gabbra had entered an age of international conference-table agreements but the Merille and the Somali had not. They raided and continue to raid the Gabbra stock freely.

The conflict has never been within the Gabbra system. The tribe's argument is with outside forces. Not for the Gabbra the indulgence of family feuds or animosity between age groups. Better to present a united front to the enemy – be it drought, famine, flood, pestilence, or hostile neighbours. Unity is still survival.

Water is all important to the Gabbra. Top: a thirsty goat at a watering-hole in the Chalbi Desert helps itself to a drink. Left: a camel train loaded with water vessels picks its way through the stony unyielding ground.

Above: A herdsman bails water into a drinking trough.

Previous page: A young Gabbra herdboy tends goats on the shores of Lake Turkana near Alia Bay. Gabbra start work as early as the age of seven and do not retire from active labour until they become old men.

Camels have been nicknamed ships of
the desert. Here a Gabbra family treks
through the badlands, homes packed
aboard the swaying beasts.

Overleaf: A Gabbra camel train passes
through a valley in the Huri Hills. The
search for water can cover hundreds of
miles over many days of bush and
desert travel.

Opposite: Already a veteran of the desert and its hardships, this young Gabbra herdboy is responsible for much of his family's stock.

Above: Permanent watering places are few – and always crowded. But arguments are rare. The Gabbra have learned the essence of co-operative living out of centuries of difficulty and danger.

Right: This family are loading water vessels onto their camel before returning to their village.

Overleaf: A Gabbra nomad strides through the wilderness on his way to Sibilot Dima Springs.

RENDILLE

The Fearless Wanderers

THE RENDILLE'S INDIFFERENCE TO SOCIAL AND ECONOMIC PROGRESS
is legendary. Their traditions – which include ritual infanticide under certain
circumstances – endure because they refuse to allow their erosion.

It was not until 1921 that the Kenyan administration attempted to govern the
tribe at all. The move was not welcomed. 'Rendille chiefs and headmen,' reported
one frustrated European official, 'are consistently inferior . . . one does not expect
much, one gets less, but they are wild people and have been taught little of the
world and its ways'.

'At first during the 1920s,' writes anthropologist Paul Spencer in *Nomads in*

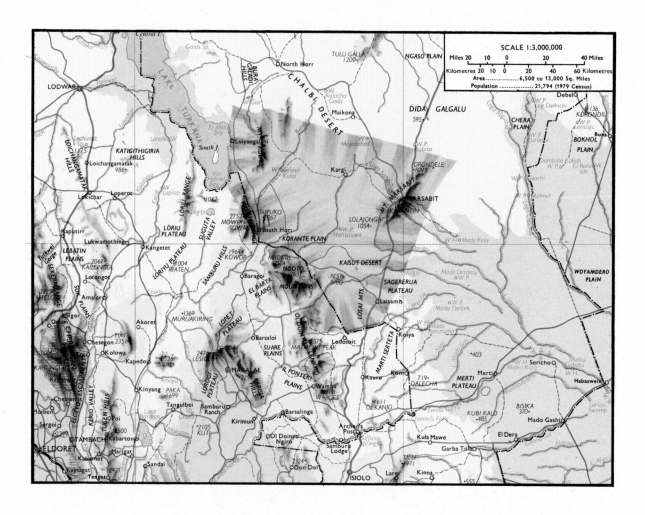

Previous page: A Rendille elder with
ears pierced for ornamentation.

Alliance, 'there was some attempt to encourage the Rendille to develop so as to bring them more into line with the other tribes of Kenya: otherwise it was felt they would be relegated to a second-class tribe. However the response from the Rendille to each new attempt varied from complete disinterest to considerable hostility'.

There were two objections: the colonial system of taxation, and forced labour for road-building. This socially sophisticated, commercially unmotivated society objected to any form of regimentation. They refused to allow anybody to trample over their intricate community or to discard their family system.

The subversive alien philosophy was treated with indifference. Through this indifference the Rendille have remained free to live their uncompromising life.

It is a life style with a touch of aristocracy about it. It puts great emphasis on single marriages and hereditary claims. The eldest son inherits the family property. The system means that the sons lower down the line of succession cannot usually hope to marry more than once. The reason for this is that the Rendille bride price is fixed at eight camels, a handsome sum these days, and the heir apparent rarely allows his brothers more than the price of one bride. 'The Rendille themselves,' says Spencer, 'point out that the customs and beliefs associated with certain forms of infanticide are related to the secret jealousy of all young brothers who can never wholly accept the total inequality of their inheritance . . . it is said that when a Rendille dies, his brother cries with one eye and counts the stock he hopes to inherit with the other.'

The inequality is accepted with resignation. Some younger brothers may leave the tribe to set up their own homestead but most remain in the hope the eldest-born will provide a heifer camel with which they can start their own herd. The attitude of acceptance is governed by the Rendille insistence that the family herd remains intact in the sole ownership of one man.

Truly pastoral, the Rendille share a common territorial boundary with the Samburu in the region of the Ol Doinyo Lenkiyo, Ndoto, and Nyiru mountains, ranging from there through the Kaisut to the south-east shores of Lake Turkana and across to Marsabit. Just how large a territory the Rendille control is uncertain. Some researchers say the 22,000-strong tribe covers an area of roughly 6,500 square miles; others claim they are spread out over as much as 13,000 square miles.

Much of this loosely-defined territory lies lower than 2,000 feet above sea level. It is arid and semi-arid with an annual rainfall which rarely exceeds seven inches. This harsh terrain makes herding an arduous and sometimes dangerous task.

Children are apprenticed into this task from the time they walk until they are 13. After that age they are allowed out on their own with the family assets.

THE EARLY years in the company of seniors also serve as an education in the values of Rendille society. The fledgling herdsman comes to understand and cherish tribal ideals and folklore. At 13, youth has already learned to conform. There are few delinquents.

Rendille education takes place in a large settlement almost invariably made up of one clan. The seniors co-operate together in economic, judicial and political affairs. Entrance to adult society is symbolised by undergoing the ritual of circumcision.

Ideally, all the initiates are circumcised together, the ceremony taking place in a settlement specially prepared by each clan. Kinfolk and elders bring gifts of new mats, precious articles in Rendille society. The gifts form the fabric of the house in which the initiates live. It is called 'The White House'.

The young men gather outside on the day of the ceremony to be initiated in turn. Each candidate is given one heifer camel for his pains. Custom demands he should now rise. Tradition decrees he remains seated – in the hope kinfolk will be generous and bestow more gifts upon him for his valiant demeanour during his ordeal. Once he walks away he acknowledges that he can accept no more.

'Rise, young man,' exhort some elders.

'Be seated,' cry some others. 'Give him more. He has been good. He has earned.'

'No – go,' shout the opposition. They are his kinfolk.

'Stay,' command the second group. 'He has herded the beasts well. We commend him. Give to him.'

The exuberance is joyful. The banter is jolly. It is an honourable festival. In the shadows the apprehensive candidate who is next in line silently urges the stubborn new-born man to move. Eventually his time comes and then it is his turn to sit as the air fills with cries in his favour, and against him.

One year later the same group assembles on the shores of Lake Turkana. It is the time of the *galgulumi*: they are to be given their age-set name.

The camp in which they live forms a circle of houses. The radius is two miles. Within the circle of houses is a circle of stones. The bowl from which they drink milk must not be touched with the hands. The cloth they wear is white and covers only their loins.

Their navels can barely be seen. The skin around each is decorated with scarification which has healed since their fathers made the incisions years ago, when they were eight or nine. Some of the young men, however, wear their loin cloth high enough to cover the navel altogether. Perhaps the scars did not heal well. And this is the time to pick out a pretty girl. Unsightly scars shame the bearer. If they are discovered he will be showered with insults which may provoke a fight.

'The worst possible insult,' says Spencer, 'would be to say to him: "You commit incest with your sister."' The tradition is obscure. Spencer, who lived with the Samburu for five years, was unable to trace its origins.

It is the only shadow which clouds this long drawn-out celebration of feasting and dancing and bathing in Lake Turkana. Spirits are high and young girls tease the warriors, flirting, precocious, darting away. Down on the shore there is the sound of laughter, a flurry of bodies, suddenly a scream as a brave snatches away a skirt.

'In a more extreme instance,' says Spencer, 'this horseplay may lead to the rape of a young girl although bodily violence on her should be avoided once her breasts have developed.' At no time should the rough and tumble involve a bride. When a girl is married joking should be confined to swearing and hurling abuse.

The girls are allied to the tribe's three age-set lines, one of which is called *sabade*. For them, the joys of love will be all too brief. It is decreed they cannot marry until all the brothers of all the girls within the age-set are married. They will remain spinsters until near, or beyond, the end of their reproductive life. They can take a lover but they cannot give birth and, if necessary, resort to abortion.

Each year Rendille families reunite at four festivals held in sequences of two. The kinfolk tending the herds at the temporary camps in the desert return to the permanent home to feast and dance.

Each family presents a beast for slaughter, the elders dipping their staves in the blood to smear it on their bodies and those of the nearby beasts.

The family is an inviolate structure to the Rendille. The elegant cockscombs the mothers wear testify to its strength and endurance. These ornaments are fashioned when the family heir is born and only removed when a direct male relative – husband or son – dies.

The mother is the focus of Rendille attention, while amongst the Samburu, warriors get the limelight. Despite this opposing emphasis the two tribes remain in close alliance. The Ariaal Rendille claim descent from both. Many Rendille young brothers migrate to the Samburu. They hope, by so doing, to establish their own independence and herds.

And there is much intermarriage. Rendille culture creates a surplus of potential brides for Samburu elders seeking to increase their prestige.

Wherever one looks in the two societies there is contradiction combined with amicability. 'There are frequent disputes caused by Rendille claiming Samburu grazing but there is seldom any serious quarrelling,' said one report. 'Relations . . . are excellent,' said another. 'Their respective elders always happily settle any minor arguments that may arise on the border.'

Perhaps the clearest distinction between the two tribes rests in their attitudes to give and take. The Samburu look for profit from a loan. The Rendille do not.

THE SPIRIT of Africa is exemplified by its tradition of hospitality. The peaceful stranger who attends an unknown village is welcomed with an openness that overwhelms. There are paradoxes here too. The poorer the home, the poorer the person, the richer the welcome. Amongst the poorest, the Rendille are perhaps the most generous – particularly to their own.

Tradition makes a niggard of the Rendille man who refuses the loan of a heifer camel to any of his tribe who ask it. It is an honour to oblige. There is prestige to be gained. But the result is ironic. Some of the richest stock-holders in Rendille society do not own a single animal outright, yet veritable paupers walk about with a claim to almost every herd they pass.

The country these herds roam is barren. The Rendille stockmen take their homes with them: primitive tents of skins and sticks which can be put up or taken down in minutes and mounted on their camels.

The interests of the Rendille concern the survival of their own society: an obsession with increasing their herds only in proportion to their population; a desire to overcome the liturgy of recurrent disasters which afflict desert life.

The Rendille worship a universal God called *Wak* but do not believe in an afterlife. Their God is a familiar one: he despises meanness and dishonesty, punishes the weak and the wicked, and upholds the virtuous and the strong.

At Korr, the principal Rendille village, a Catholic missionary, Father Redento Tignonsini, aspired to be the spiritual counsellor of these people for many years. He left behind the memory of a good man. Indeed he turned the village of Korr into an oasis, sinking eight boreholes. Living among the Rendille, just as they did, in a house of hide and grass which he built, he gained their affection, confidence and respect. Nevertheless, at the end of all his efforts he estimated that perhaps only ten out of every ten thousand Rendille had accepted the Christian faith. He would be glad to know that he is still remembered – and missed.

Today, in modern Kenya, Rendille society remains inviolate – but for how long no-one can predict. African cultures have suffered swifter erosion and greater pressures than those in almost any other part of the world and over a shorter period of time. In some parts of the continent the results are alarming. There is confusion and despair, political corruption, social alienation and humiliation.

The Rendille have not yet suffered this fate. It might not be asking too much to let them maintain their society as it is.

Following pages: Early morning in the
Kaisut Desert as a Rendille camel herd is
taken out for grazing.

Left: The village of Korr is little more than a scattering of domes of hides and sticks and grass. For the Rendille, happiness is measured by matters less material than the elegance of a home.

Above: From time immemorial the game of *bao* has dominated leisure activities in East and Central Africa. It is a game of great skill and formalised rituals.

Left: The Rendille Chief at Korr, Chief Jeiso Wambile.

Above left: A youngster is served with milk from a handmade container. Rendille families are loving and close-knit units but the tribe does not allow population to expand more quickly than their herds.

Left: This tubby youngster in a Rendille village seems to thoroughly enjoy the desert life.

Above: Two young children pause to work out the best way to move a water-tight container nearer home.

Rendille, like many other pastoralists, relish the blood of their stock mixed with milk. The technique for drawing camel's blood is very similar to that used by the Samburu and Turkana tribes to draw blood from their cattle stock. The beast chosen to be the donor is forced to kneel, and a helper knots a thong around its neck, causing the jugular vein to bulge. Another tribesman shoots an arrow into the jugular from close range and the blood starts to pump in powerful jets. An out-turned palm deflects the flow downward into the container in which the blood is collected before being mixed with milk.

Left: The elegant cockscomb signifies that this proud beauty is married and has already given birth to an heir. The cockscomb is braided at the birth of her first-born son – and only removed after the death of either her husband or her son.

Top right: A variation on the cockscomb, plastered solid with mud, which signifies the same status.

Top left: In the village of Korr, a mother helps to adjust her daughter's ostrich eggshell necklace.

Above and right: Although culturally close to the Samburu, Rendille warriors wear longer hair and a different style of robe.

Overleaf: A Rendille camel herd returning towards the home village after watering.

EL-MOLO

Hunters of the Jade Sea

NO SMALLER GROUP IN THE WORLD HAS RECEIVED SO MUCH ATTENTION
as the 400 or so el-Molo who live in a litter of dome-shaped reed dwellings on the
south-east shore of Lake Turkana.

Their past is shrouded in folklore, legend and mystery. Their future as a
resident group on the lake's edge is uncertain. All they own are their few fragile
homes. They believe, too, that all the fish, hippo and crocodile which live in the
lake belong to them.

It would be foolish to tell them that the lake's life is not theirs. They would not
listen. The el-Molo have lived by the water from time unknown, long before
Count Teleki and von Hohnel reached the shore.

'Almost at the last gasp, we hastened on towards the slightly rippled sheet of
water – the one bit of brightness in a gloomy scene. Another hour of tramping

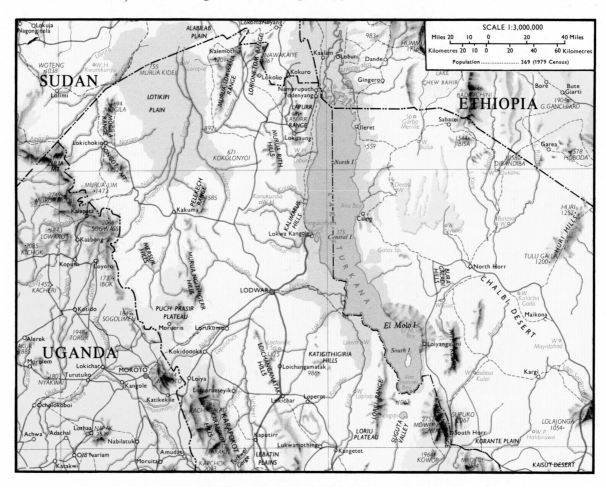

Previous page: The cow-rib ear-ring
signifies that this el-Molo hunter has
harpooned a hippo.

through sand or over stony flats, and we were at the shore of the lake. Although utterly exhausted after the seven hours march in the intense and parching heat, we felt our spirits rise once more as we stood upon the beach at last and saw the beautiful water, clear as crystal, stretching away before us.'

The members of Teleki's party were dehydrated and were disappointed to find that the lake's water was bitter and soda laden. 'This fresh defeat of all our expectations was like a revelation to us: and like some threatening spectre rose up before our minds the full significance of the utterly barren, dreary nature of the lake district.'

Yet the el-Molo have lived here for centuries, prey to much greater misfortune, especially disease and attack by stronger tribes. They suffer an ill-balanced diet – too much protein-rich fish, too much fluoride, too much water, too little relief from their arid land base. Bandy-legged, tooth-stained, they nevertheless impress all who meet them. 'I felt,' said Hillaby, 'as if we had stumbled on a race that had survived simply because Time had forgotten to finish them off'.

This Neolithic life-style has fascinated all who have encountered it in the last century. But it has not helped outsiders to understand the el-Molo. Their name and origins remain subjects of confused conjecture; a confusion which has been compounded by basic difficulties of communication, the tribe's dependence on an oral history enriched with each retelling, and a lack of appreciation of their individual identity by earlier visitors.

Credence has been given to the assumption they are the smallest tribe in Africa, if not the world, and in danger of extinction.

'Whether the el-Molo are in fact the smallest tribe in Africa or even Kenya,' comments Spencer, 'must largely depend on one's definition of tribe.' He argued they were substantially the same as other groups elsewhere. When he visited them in 1958 his census established a population of 143 persons living in two villages three miles apart. The figure has increased dramatically since then due mainly to intermarriage with the Samburu.

'In 1958,' records Spencer, 'the only newcomers to the el-Molo in living memory had been three Turkana men. No woman had been married into the tribe from elsewhere, although one or two of their women had been married off.'

The el-Molo are basically monogamous, although Spencer found a 'rather forceful Turkana' had taken more than one wife. They differ from their neighbours the Samburu, too, in regard to morality. Sexual relations before marriage are deplored.

The el-Molo ability to adapt to circumstance is astonishing. In half a century, for example, their language has changed completely. 'In 1958,' notes Spencer, 'the oldest living men only remembered words of their old language, middle-aged men only knew that there had been another language, while a number of younger men were not even aware of this fact'.

The most favoured conjecture about the el-Molo's origin is that they are a remnant Rendille group who took to fishing for survival. Both Rendille and el-Molo worship a God called *Wak*; they observe many common cultural habits – for example, burying their dead under stone cairns. More important, at the start of the twentieth century they had a common language.

THE NAME the el-Molo use for themselves is *el-Des*. It is believed the title el-Molo may have derived from two possible misunderstandings. When von Hohnel asked their name he was pointing to a man fishing and was told: '*ol-Moruo*' – a Cushitic word to describe a fisherman. However, a similar-sounding word from which el-Molo might possibly derive – given vowel distortion – is the Maasai, *Il-Torobo*.

In the sociological science of the twentieth century the Bantu corruption of the word, *Ndorobo*, has come to mean remnants of tribes who, for some reason, have abandoned pastoralism in favour of survival by hunting and gathering.

The word has contemptuous overtones. In the eyes of the Maasai for example, there is considerable stigma in being a *Ndorobo*. This attitude exists amongst the Samburu too.

Ndorobo groups are distinguished by hunting wild animals for meat, and gathering honey. Essentially this is what the el-Molo do – although the wild beasts they hunt are aquatic – crocodile and hippo – and they gather not honey but fish.

El-Molo fishermen ride on doum-palm log rafts that quickly absorb water and float just beneath the surface when loaded with nets and crew. The heron-like poise of the el-Molo fisherman as he stands motionless with his quivering harpoon of hardened thorn-tree root, detachable barbed tip glinting as the sun strikes the metal, is unforgettable.

Seen in silhouette on these ancient vessels, the el-Molo swiftly spear Nile perch and tilapia with an iron-age dexterity that deceives the eye. But extreme caution is required. Within seconds fearsome gales can whip round the 7,500-foot mass of nearby Mount Kulal to churn the lake into a deadly swell. Few navigators can ride out such a storm and it sometimes happens that the bulky, uncontrollable rafts are swept out into the mainstream of the lake, their crews never to be seen again.

Such tragedies strike the small community hard.

HARPOONS ARE one of the three types of el-Molo implement. The others are hook and line, and netting. More recently they have adopted the basket trap used by those Turkana who have turned to fishing.

The el-Molo make their ropes from the fibre of the thorn tree. The harpoon haft is seasoned from acacia roots. Dried in the sun, this haft is smeared with fat by the tribe's smiths and heated over a camp fire for shaping. Heated iron cauterises the hole for the metal head.

Harpoons specifically for hippo-hunting, however, are made with a stronger haft – fashioned out of oryx horn seared by a heated spear blade to make an opening for the metal tip.

Only one or two el-Molo are skilled smiths. They forge their lethal implements from scraps of iron which they heat in a dung fire before hammering them into shape. As well as harpoons and hooks, they fashion the axes with which the tribe hack down the ubiquitous doum palm to make their porous rafts. Women work the fibre of the doum palm leaves to make fishing nets.

Unlike any of their neighbours the el-Molo depend almost entirely on the lake and they understand its ways. There is perhaps some basis for the story that no crocodile ever attacks an el-Molo. The tribe, however, hunts crocodile – especially when the desire for a change from the monotonous diet of fish and turtle and crocodile eggs overwhelms them.

The saurians lie sunbathing in profusion, some half-submerged, in the cloudy lagoons which abound on the shores north of Loiyangalani. These shores are sometimes used to water the Rendille and Samburu herds and every so often an unsuspecting goat or sheep is taken by a crocodile. More rarely, an unwary herdsman, or woman filling gourds with water, may vanish silently into the deep.

Crocodiles strike swiftly and ferociously. Yet the el-Molo enter the waters fearlessly. In living history, not a single tribesman has been taken.

The el-Molo attack is simple in its execution. The hunting group slips quietly into the shallows. Using reeds for cover they move out into the lake, before turning downwind and slowly inshore to stalk the victim they have spotted lying up in the reeds.

Suddenly, not more than thirty feet from the half-dozing monster, the waters erupt as the el-Molo warriors dash forward, harpoons whistling through the air.

The reptile's body coils in pain as the points pierce its corrugated hide. The tail whip-lashes. The long snout, articulated, gapes open, snapping shut in a futile attempt to seize its tormentors. Snarled in rope, the crocodile is hauled into the shallows where its spine is severed with downward jabs of an el-Molo spear.

The best cuts, the fatty tail and tongue, are grilled on the shore to revive the exultant hunters. The rest of the carcase is butchered. The cuts are laid out to dry in the sun. Later, wrapped in reeds, they are carried back to the village.

HIPPO HUNTING is a more profound activity both because it is more complex and because el-Molo legend has it that the tribe once held large herds of domestic stock but that these were hippo, crocodile, and turtle which one day wandered into the lake in search of an old woman's pot – and were lost forever.

Their hunting of these lost beasts is restricted these days. Hippos, like crocodile, are a protected species in Kenya. Furthermore, hereditary intuition has given the hippo a sense that the beaches around el-Molo villages are unsafe. They have moved far north. Preparations for hunting them therefore take some time to organise. A long march is also involved – to half-way between el-Molo Bay and Alia Bay.

When they reach the right spot the hunters lie up all day concealed in the reeds as close to the hippo colony as discretion allows. The leader of the group plans the stalk efficiently, pointing out landmarks and the victim selected for slaughter. It is often late at night when the scout checking the herd's slow progress from the deep water to the shore – where the hippos will browse until dawn – gives the signal for the attack to start.

The victim is usually a semi-mature calf. Sometimes its parents and companions will charge the hunters. But the el-Molo are fully in control.

The night fills with boastful cries and the songs of blooded warriors. The young beast is finished off with a spear, then left to lie on its back in the shallows until the morning. The hunters keep vigil the night long singing a chant of victory.

In the morning, the beast is hauled ashore and the lead harpoonist mounts its neck. The tongue is cut out and draped around him. His body is daubed on either side with red and white patterns of clay and he starts to sing – a long, moaning pulsating and wordless drone of triumph which continues all day as the beast is butchered and sun dried before the long journey home.

Back in the village the harpoonist is a hero and the hippo's tail, ears and lips are displayed outside his hut. He is praised and the tribe jubilant.

Days later the hero returns to the lake shore and throws the trophies which were hanging outside his hut back into the water.

FEWER THAN half a million people inhabit the vast wildernesses around Lake Turkana. And by the turn of the century more Kenyans will live in cities than in the countryside.

Alone among the world's species, mankind has learned to control his own reproduction yet he is not diminishing. Arguably, however, his cultures are, and his productive land, too.

The only other creature which destroys its natural habitat is the elephant which is now on the way to extinction, with mankind's help of course. Once it was feared this would be the fate of the Hunters of the Jade Sea.

The el-Molo are not going to be wiped out, but their culture is vanishing quickly. Improved social facilities, the evangelical mission of the Consolata Catholic Fathers and Loiyangalani primary school have all quickened the pace of change.

This has led to an understandable but misplaced fear among some ethnographers that el-Molo society is changing too swiftly. In general, this is true of many groups in Africa which are being swept into the alien and amorphous cities with harsh cultural consequences. For their size the el-Molo are particularly vulnerable.

But unlike the other groups the el-Molo are ethnically indistinct. 'The ethnographer,' says anthropologist Edmund Leach, 'has often only managed to discern the existence of "a tribe" because he took it as axiomatic that this kind of cultural identity must exist. Many such tribes, in a sense, are ethnographic fiction.'

For the el-Molo this must surely be the case. They are a tribe in name only, and so perhaps for them alone the pace of change on the shores of the Jade Sea, near the 'Cradle of Mankind', is not yet fast enough.

Right: A young el-Molo
prepares to cast for fish in the jade
waters of Lake Turkana.

Above: The comparative calm of el-Molo Bay demonstrates the productivity of the tribe's most trusted fishing method. The dragnet is carried out to the shallows by family groups in the quiet of the early morning. Several dozen good-sized tilapia and other species are driven into the encircling net by the team of men, women and youngsters.

Left: Finishing off a netted fish with the sharp end of an oryx horn.

Opposite: The el-Molo's centuries-old fishing techniques have recently been supplemented by basket traps introduced from the Turkana tribe for catching bottom fish in muddy, reedy areas.

Above: Balanced on a ponderous doum-palm raft this young el-Molo fisherman triumphantly harpoons a fish.

Right: Up to his waist in water this el-Molo fisherman retrieves a valuable harpoon head. His ear-ring, made from cow rib-bone, is proof he has killed a hippo. Married women wear the same ear-ring to show their status.

Hippos, like this one found offshore below Moiti Hill, are said by the el-Molo to be part of their lost wandering herds. Hunting is planned according to tribal legends and traditions and has a spiritual quality not without its risks. Enraged, the hippo is perhaps the most dangerous of all African game. Nevertheless, hours before, these el-Molo hunters had plunged into the dark night waters of the lake, in a violent swell, to mark out their victim. After the kill it was towed inshore to rest overnight in the shallows, legs upwards. In the morning the hunter whose harpoon was the first to hit hauls the beast ashore assisted by a colleague.

The hero of the night's hunt sits astride the carcase as his colleagues butcher the beast (opposite). The moment is spiritual, a redemption, by traditional means alone, of a beast that belongs to the tribe. The hunters chant a liturgy of triumph to celebrate the kill. The singing started when the first harpoon was removed from the body – the moment regarded as the symbolic time of death. The final cuts remove the trophies – the ears, tongue and tail – which are fastened to the hero's harpoon.

Below: The balance of the meat is cut into thin strips and laid over brushwood to dry in the sun. Later it is wrapped in reed bundles and carried back to the village.

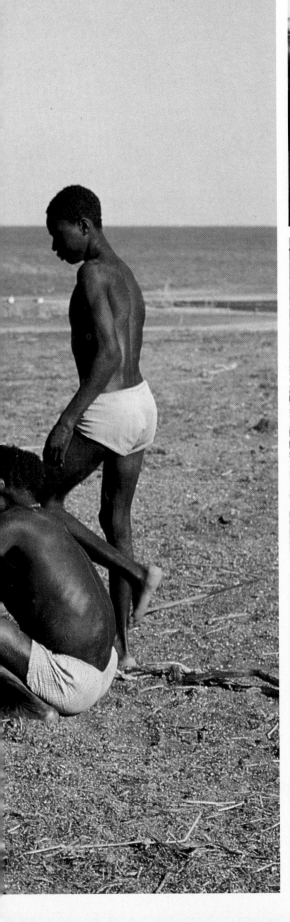

Above: It takes skill to spear crocodile from such a fragile raft.

Left: The young reptile is quickly hauled aboard. Small crocodiles are speared from rafts, larger ones are hunted on foot.

Right: Crocodile breakfasts are a rare delicacy. This eager youngster trots triumphantly home with his surprise treat for the family.

Top: Children watch in anticipation as their mother prepares crocodile for the pot. The el-Molo subsist on a protein-rich diet of fish, and alkaline water, which causes certain physical defects. Crocodile meat is therefore relished as a change from the boredom of the monotonous fish diet.

Above: A Nile perch bone makes a useful spoon.

Right: The domed huts of the el-Molo village on el-Molo Island. In the foreground are the tribe's burial cairns.

Above: The people of el-Molo Island pose for a group picture.

Opposite top left: The el-Molo make fibre for nets, mats, clothes and rope from doum palm leaves which are left to soften in the lake and later pounded between two stones to separate the fibres. The girl is weaving a rug from these fibres.

Opposite top right: Lattice work of bare thorn-tree branches provides raw material for a family hut.

Opposite bottom left: Potters' skills are passed on within families. Only a few el-Molo now have the knowledge to make traditional pottery. It is prepared by moulding local clay into successive layers before burnishing with a short, wooden stick and then air drying. Baking later in a dung fire lasts less than an hour.

Opposite bottom right: The pottery has a plain functional beauty and serves its purpose well.

Top: The hunters wade swift-foot through the ruffled shallows, harpoons at the ready.

Above: el-Molo stalk crocodiles on foot in the reedy shallows north of el-Molo Bay. They move in with unerring sureness until the giant reptiles are unable to escape. Enmeshed in rope, stung by the pain of the embedded harpoon, this snapping crocodile vainly tries to free itself and turn on its tormentors.

Right: Articulated jaws snapping in reflex, a mature Nile crocodile, member of a species which has lived in Lake Turkana for more than 130 million years, struggles furiously to free itself.

Right: At the end of the hunt, repeated downward spear jabs sever the reptile's spinal cord. Below: the crocodile is dragged away to the camp. Opposite: glowing coals roast the succulent meat for the feast which follows the hard day's hunt.

Overleaf: el-Molo – time for transition.

JOURNEY
AROUND THE
JADE SEA

A JOURNEY TO LAKE TURKANA IS AN experience of time removed; but whether of time removed to the past or to the future, I am not sure.

The usual association is with the pre-historic, with the image of Richard Leakey's '1470' hominid, remote ancestor of the human race. But that picture shows a lush, jungly landscape, and this is not Turkana. Nothing like it.

It is the most bleak and arid of future perspectives. A land devastated, raked by some monstrous heat; defoliated, cauterised and burned to cinder and grey ash over large areas. Life persists, but not much of it, and at the lowest conceivable level.

From the deck of a fishing-boat anchored at Alia Bay, the unblinking eyes of a sleeping crocodile reflected red in the beam of a torch. The reptile might be the emblem species of Turkana, a survivor for 130 million years, but maybe for not much longer.

Another red beacon in the darkness was the flicker of a dung fire on the mainland. Probably el-Molo, another relic species at Turkana and also perhaps destined for extinction in the advance of modern man from the south.

I had this inevitability in mind on my first trip to the lake in 1968, co-incidentally the year that progenitor man was discovered at Koobi Fora. I began photographing the people and the landscape for a personal record of vanishing Africa. The conception of a public record, a book, came later after many more visits.

In 1979, the book was close to completion, but there were gaps. Nothing on the Suguta Valley in the south, and nothing on the Omo across the northern border in Ethiopia. Hence the idea of an expedition, the first motor safari round the lake.

Previous page: The Turkana Expedition pick-up races behind the lead vehicle in the alluvial dust bed of Suguta Valley.

There were months of preparation, not least a protracted negotiation with the Ethiopian authorities in Addis Ababa for permission to cross the Omo River.

Once that problem had been overcome others arose. One was time: six weeks was as much as I could spend on the journey. Secondly, there were no precedents on which to draw, no-one else's experience of a similar four-wheel-drive expedition to learn from. Thirdly, the area is remote and there are risks in travelling through it – a lack of drinking water and, of course, no medical facilities at all. Fourthly, combined with the natural hazards of a desert environment, were the added perils of stumbling upon marauding bandits or becoming lost or stranded.

In country like Turkana, it is essential to travel with reliable people whose skills and temperaments complement one another. Next to cost, therefore, deciding the composition of the five-man team was the factor which occupied me most.

The criterion for selection was my personal knowledge of each team member. They had to be people who could live together in the bush without too much friction, basically cut off from any other contact for several weeks.

The final line-up was Stewart Sommerlad, a tough Australian radio correspondent with a strong mechanical streak, Andrew Johnson, a young British graduate and a veteran of several expeditions, Brian Tetley, and two other long-time Kenya friends – journalist Peter Moll and Saidi Suleiman Salim, my personal assistant, both past members of many of my Turkana safaris.

They were with me when I went to see Noel Kennaway in a suburb of Nairobi for advice on the route plan.

Forty years before, he had been the District Officer of the area in which the lake lies and he knew as much about Suguta and the other tougher parts of the region as any man alive. 'Nobody's ever driven around it by road,' he added. 'There is just no way. It is impossible.'

The route I chose ran through Nyahururu, Rumuruti, Maralal, Baragoi, on to the west flank of Mount Nyiru to Tum and from there down through Parkati into the Suguta Valley, then around the Loriu Plateau and through the Kerio Valley to Kalokol which lies near Ferguson's Gulf. Beyond lay Namuruputh and the unknown element of Ethiopia, its border post and guards, and the Omo, perhaps the most uncertain factor in the entire journey. Not even the Ethiopian authorities we asked knew if there was any ferry to carry the vehicles across. In comparison with all this, the second half of the journey down the eastern shore, if we ever reached there, looked as if it would be an anti-climax.

For more than half a century, largely during colonial times, the whole Lake Turkana region was a closed zone kept isolated from the rest of the country and patrolled by troops. Whatever the motives for this policy, it had the effect of insulating the peoples of the lake, and their traditions, from the changes going on around them. This is no longer true today. Modern Kenya wants all its citizens to have equal access to the benefits of development. This is a good philosophy, but inevitably it has its negative aspects. Around Lake Turkana it has meant that many old customs are being swept aside, perhaps too quickly.

The Samburu circumcision ceremony, for instance, is unlikely to occur again on the scale I witnessed. Fourteen years elapse between each ceremony, and by the time the next is due we may have seen the transformation of this region and of such rituals – events which go back literally hundreds of years unchanged in all their essential detail and meaning.

While features of the old ways remain, therefore, the challenge to record them is irresistible – although this is no easy task. In remote areas, people are intensely suspicious of all outsiders. Some even believe the camera taking the picture is stealing their soul.

Kenya is my home, though, and I know it well, particularly the desert lands in the north, and I can communicate fluently with nearly all Kenyans, mostly in Swahili.

Over the years that I have been visiting Lake Turkana I have made friends with a number of chiefs and village elders and we have come to trust one another. I have had

A team member guides the tow boat and ferry on the perilous crossing of Omo River. The station wagon sways precariously aboard a jury-rigged pontoon which was swept away by the current when the engine failed.

some remarkable co-operation during my photographic sessions from people whom I have also seen being decidedly hostile to camera-carrying strangers.

My budget for the expedition ran into thousands of pounds. Equipment included a station wagon and a pick-up, both with four-wheel drive, and a 250cc trailbike for path-finding. There were also three custom-built tents complete with accessories – foam mattresses, two gas cookers, a refrigerator, and a petrol-driven generator. Other items included twenty eight-ply tyres, 800 litres of petrol, 275 litres of drinking water, basic rations for the trip, a quarter-ton of photographic equipment and film, and half-a-ton of spares for mechanical collapse, if and when it came. For communications we carried a 900-mile range radio telephone. To get us through especially difficult terrain we also carried a power-winch, sand-ladders and three-foot Tanganyika jacks. I had also hoped to take an inflatable dinghy with outboard motor for puttering around near the shores of the lake, but at the last minute this and other stores, including food, were left out because there was just no more room.

The day before departure was spent loading the vehicles. Priorities were established – and supplies not needed immediately were stored in Nairobi. A light plane would meet us at various locations to bring in replenishments, or at least that was the plan. Three airlifts were arranged but in the event we only needed one, at Ferguson's Gulf.

The expedition finally set off at midnight on Thursday January 17, 1980, one vehicle leaving about twenty minutes ahead of mine. We linked up in the highland town of Nyahururu, formerly Thomson's Falls, just after two in the morning and refuelled.

North from Nyahururu there was nothing but dirt road, and after Tum, no road at all. Our route led through Rumuruti, a ranching town, and then on to Maralal. Just a mile out of Rumuruti, however, my overloaded station wagon rolled, injuring Brian Tetley, who was sent to a Nairobi hospital. The vehicle was severely damaged. All the bodywork was tilted to one side, with both front doors bent askew and the front passenger area pushed inwards. All the windows were shattered.

Andrew Johnson wrote up the accident in the expedition log:

'It seems, on reflection, that the great weight on

the roof – jerricans of petrol, tyres, tents, et al. – slung the vehicle outwards on a corner. It thereupon mounted a three-foot embankment, felled a telegraph pole and rolled over on the left side.'

We took stock for twenty-four hours at Nyahururu, repaired what we could and hammered the worst protruberances back into the body-work. More equipment including a tent, beds and the refrigerator had to be jettisoned.

But there were minor compensations. The lack of windscreen and windows, for instance, provided welcome ventilation when we eventually reached the Suguta Valley. A precipitous track, hand-made by an Italian missionary, leads down from Parkati for a few miles before petering out. And it was along these boulder-strewn slopes, forty-eight hours later, that the much lighter station wagon crept into the valley, surely one of the hottest places on earth. From now on we became trail-blazers in the truest sense of the word.

Our two vehicles trailed a great cloud of dust as they raced across the floor of the

The author with his camera equipment at the Expedition's Alia Bay camp.

Suguta Valley. The dried-up mud flats which we had to cross had turned into a giant shimmering saucepan. They divide the two lakes, Logipi and Alablab. Ahead lay Nadikum where we planned to camp. The spot was marked on our map as a water hole but when we reached this grove of doum palms in the heart of the valley there was no water, only shade.

We stayed in the Suguta for four days, braising slowly in our own sweat at noon temperatures of up to 137 degrees Fahrenheit. While there we climbed a perfect cone of ash called 'Andrew's Volcano', named after Lieutenant H. Andrew, a member of the Cavendish expedition to Turkana in 1897. Another climb, more rewarding, was across The Barrier, the coal-black crust of a vast lava flow which prevents just about any form of access to the southern tip of Turkana. But we saw it from there, the beautiful Siren in jade. Perhaps not quite that dangerous, but often menacing and obviously feminine.

The smooth cones and the soft sand-spit curves of the bay are definitive. In its benign mood, a dense mass of blue-green algae is still and the facet of jade image is precisely right. As it happened it was steel-blue when we saw it from the ridge of The Barrier. A moderate wind was being sucked in from somewhere out beyond Mt. Kulal, the surface water churned, and the lake assumed the grey, sombre, sullen or brooding aspect of Jade Sea literature.

At some point in the day, the intake of air into the lake basin becomes frantic, as though Turkana is gasping for breath. This is the violent mood; the phenomenon of the roaring gales which fog the land with ash and dust and batter the human intruder. In this state, the lake is dangerous, as Alistair Graham recorded – vindictive, vicious and potentially a killer. Anyone who has been in the area has seen this savage nature under the superficial beauty. More than a few people have been fatal casualties of the encounter.

Our climbs proved what we already knew – that there was no way to drive over The Barrier to the Kerio Valley.

So we returned to the Suguta, which as it happens is one of the more interesting of the Turkana landscapes. The shallow pan of 'Lake' Alablab and its bigger sister Logipi still had a filling of pink soda slush, like rotting confectionery.

The fringes of the lakes are treacherous for anything but the splay-footed flamingoes, thousands of which were dipping into the scummy water and draining off the algae on which they subsist. The lakes are fed by hot springs, and there are stories of wandering tribesmen falling through the brittle mud crust into a boiling pool.

We decided to move on as directly as possible from the Suguta to Kalokol halfway along the western shore of Lake Turkana. We estimated that the journey would take us two days. We could not afford to take much longer since our supply of water was already running low.

Two nights later, in fast-gathering darkness, we pitched camp as the sun sank behind a low hill. We had winched our way over screes and rocks and spent back-breaking hours clearing boulders from our path and, encouraged by our Turkana guides, had continued into a rugged wilderness. And now we were quite lost. What had begun as an adventure had turned into an ordeal of dehydration and energy-sucking heat, fatigue and bewilderment. The guides we had hired finally admitted that they had no idea where we were.

Three more days passed before we finally reached Lokori, and then Kalokol near Ferguson's Gulf, the village where the Turkana Fishermen's Co-operative has brought the first signs of the industrial era to the region. A large filleting and freezing plant was nearing completion as we camped in the shade of some palms.

By now the station wagon needed a thorough repair job. Despite having taken off most of the weight, the rack was causing the roof to move around alarmingly: both front windscreen pillars had broken away and cracks were appearing around all the other pillars.

With the help of the Co-operative's mechanic, Stewart Sommerlad set to work. After almost three days the station wagon had a pipe frame that bolted to the floor in four places and also around the windscreen pillars. This kept the tottering superstructure more or less rigid and in place for the rest of the trip.

The finished product was not exactly a model construction. It was necessary to wrap a blanket around the cross bars to prevent the driver and front seat passengers from fracturing their skulls when the vehicle bounced on rough roads. Neither was the assembly a work of art; but at that stage aesthetics were of marginal concern.

It was at Ferguson's Gulf that Peter Moll

left us to return to his business and Gavin Bennett, a young journalist and a veteran of the Kenya wilds, arrived by air. The light plane also brought vital spares and carried back exposed films to Nairobi for processing.

Once reassembled, the expedition set off for an exploration of Central Island, an hour away by power-boat from Ferguson's Gulf. A still active volcano, Central Island has three craters – one large, one small and side-vented, and the third submerged as a sand-fringed lagoon. It sounds attractive, but erosion has left the island looking hardly more scenic than a colliery tip.

Central Island could erupt at any moment and, amongst other damage, wipe out an important resting place for the migrant birds which come there attracted by the fruit of bright green *salvadora* bushes. There was no indication of an impending eruption when we were there, but the birds were clearly soon going to need another place to feed since the *salvadora* is being destroyed by the fishermen who camp on the island.

Back on the main track up the western shore of the lake from Ferguson's Gulf, there was

Routes marked as motorable on Second World War survey maps have long since vanished into the Turkana wilderness. The Expedition blazed its own trails through uncharted bush.

nothing to relieve the monotony. We co-vered over a hundred miles of flattish, featureless scrub desert with nothing alive in it, or so it seemed.

It was not until after the Kenya border post at Todenyang that we were diverted by any incident of note.

The expedition had been cleared to enter Ethiopia by the highest authorities in Addis Ababa. And, just to make sure, the day before taking the expedition across I paid a visit to the Ethiopian border post at Namuruputh. I was greeted warmly and told that the expedition would be welcome. When we arrived, however, we were arres-ted – the full drama, with rifles at our backs. The letters and visas meant nothing after all.

We persuaded the border guards to let us use our radio and eventually we got through to the Ethiopian Embassy in Nairobi who contacted Addis Ababa on our behalf. The response was an order, in Amharic morse, from the Ethiopian capital to let us into their country. The performance had taken forty-eight hours.

We then drove on a few miles to what I had always considered would be the biggest obstacle in any 'grand design' to drive round Lake Turkana – the meandering waters of the River Omo, more than a quarter of a mile wide at the village of Kalaam.

In the sixties, Kalaam had been a ferry-point for crossing the Omo, the sluggish fresh-water feed for the lake. The problem was that the American missionaries who built and operated the ferry had departed when Ethiopia became a Marxist state after the overthrow of Emperor Haile Selassie. Ethiopia's new revolutionary government failed to keep the Omo ferry in working order. Thus, although originally a well-constructed unit consisting of a steel platform on top of twenty-five oil drums, it had fallen into decay. The drums had corroded into a mesh of holes and the pontoon lay half-submerged on the gentle slopes of the bank.

Hearts sinking, we drove fourteen miles upstream, directed by George Kistachir, the District Officer, to a place called Omo Rati where a second ferry was located. This turned out to be a series of planks on top of three large fibreglass dinghies. It looked solid enough, and it was floating, although a fourth dinghy was missing. The banks were steep and I worried that they might cause problems when loading and unloading. To overcome this obstacle we dug tons of earth out of the banks on both sides to make ramps.

One member of the team scrounged a broken-down outboard motor from George and managed to get it working. The rest of us set about strengthening and improving the ferry – a job that took a day and a night of hard labour, wiring oil drums and timber together. We christened the thing the 'Rati Queen' before we inched the station wagon aboard, very nearly losing it in the process. Then the unpredictable outboard seized in midstream.

The log records the historic crossing:

'Locomotion was achieved by Stewart and the towing boat and (arguably but not definitely) by ten unco-ordinated Merille lads recruited as oarsmen. When cast adrift, the ferry and contents proceeded directly up-stream since Stewart had difficulty in obtaining the purchase of engine in the water necessary for the pre-determined course. Occasionally he was able to influence the direction of the convoy which described a series of S-bends before finally arriving at the opposite bank, 400 yards further up-stream than was intended. The ferry was therefore hand-hauled to a point where the truck could be disembarked.'

The second crossing was less erratic and the pick-up was landed without mishap.

Originally we had intended to spend at least a week in Ethiopia but we were followed everywhere at gunpoint – 'for our own protection', I was assured – and repeatedly warned that photography was not allowed. So now that we had crossed the Omo I did not want to spend longer than necessary in Ethiopia. After an overnight camp on the eastern shores of the Omo I decided to head for Kenya. It was not much later, after travelling for some thirty miles on the east bank, that our two-vehicle convoy drove over a small rise and we sighted a new Ethiopian border post. This was something we had not expected. As we approached it, two soldiers came out levelling their rifles at us as they ran down the hill. They seemed to have had a message about our expected arrival for they waved vigorously, presumably directing us into the border post. However, we picked up speed and ran straight past them, over the line to Kenya and did not stop until we reached the police station at Ileret.

Thereafter, I set a leisurely pace down the lake's eastern shores. We camped at various places, including Koobi Fora where a team of scientists led by Richard Leakey has unearthed the earliest known human remains.

It took us the better part of three weeks to get that far. In all we covered around 1,800 miles of some of the toughest terrain in the world – a tangle of tracks and unmarked paths, muddled together with volcanic boulders, precipitous slopes, lava sand and scrub desert.

We really did feel as if we had achieved the impossible. The drivers were near to exhaustion after inching their way through these wildernesses at speeds no higher than fifteen miles an hour. They were tired of continually driving in low gear and fearing that the vehicles would shake to pieces, and they were strained by having to concentrate every second to avoid wrecking chassis and axles on giant boulders or driving over the edge of an abyss.

In twenty-seven days we had tracked from Maralal through the Nyiru Mountains and down into Suguta Valley, across the forbidding 4,500 feet heights of the Loriu Plateau and along the featureless desert plain through Ferguson's Gulf to Todenyang. From there we journeyed into Ethiopia and back along the rutted burnt-out plains of the eastern shore. By the time we reached Loiyangalani we were quite ready to return to the twentieth-century bustle of the Kenya capital. But first I had some friends to visit.

The el-Molo have lived near Loiyangalani for many centuries and arriving at el-Molo Bay was something of a homecoming for me.

El-Molo Bay is where I first began my 'love affair' with Lake Turkana and after many visits the tribe are old friends.

I had recorded perhaps their last hippo hunt. Their history was ending. Time has finally caught up with the people it forgot.

But I had my book, a permanent record of Lake Turkana and its people as they were.

And I had my hope: that Kenya in the rest of this century might allow this unique piece of living pre-history to retain all of its integrity and some of its mystery.

A view over slopes covered in lava sand
from the peak of Andrew's Volcano
towards the 3,500 foot mass of The Barrier.

Bibliography

Adamson, Joy, *The Peoples of Kenya*, LONDON: Collins and Harvill Press, 1967.

Barber, James, *Imperial Frontiers*, KENYA: East African Publishing House, 1969.

Cambridge, T. R., *In the Land of the Turkana*, LONDON: Heath Cranton Ltd., 1920.

Graham, Alistair and Peter Beard, *Eyelids of Morning*,
CONNECTICUT, USA, New York Graphic Society, 1973.

Gulliver, P. H., *The Family Herds*, LONDON: Routledge & Kegan Paul, 1955;
USA: Humanities Press, 1955.

Hillaby, John, *Journey to the Jade Sea*, LONDON: Constable Publishers, 1964.

Leakey, Richard and Roger Lewin, *Origins*, LONDON: Macdonald and Jane's, 1977;
NEW YORK: E. P. Dutton, 1977.

Leakey, Richard and Roger Lewin, *Peoples of the Lake*, LONDON: Collins, 1979;
NEW YORK: Doubleday, 1978.

Spencer, Paul, *Nomads in Alliance*, LONDON and NEW YORK: Oxford University Press, 1973.

Von Hohnel, Ludwig, *The Discovery of Lake Rudolf and Lake Stefanie*,
LONDON: Frank Cass, 1968.

Willock, Colin, *Africa's Rift Valley*, LONDON and NEW YORK: Time-Life Books, 1974.